Securing U.S. Energy Supplies

Securing U.S. Energy Supplies

The Private Sector as an Instrument of Public Policy

William G. Prast
Atlantis Energy and Mineral
Economic Services, Inc.

Lexington Books
D.C. Heath and Company
Lexington, Massachusetts
Toronto

cap. A

Library of Congress Cataloging in Publication Data

Prast, William G
    Securing U.S. energy supplies.

    1. Energy policy—United States.   2. Power resources—United
States.   I. Title.
HD9502.U52P7   333.79′11′0973   79-2978
ISBN 0-669-03305-7

Copyright © 1981 by D.C. Heath and Company

Published simultaneously in Canada

Printed in the United States of America.

International Standard Book Number: 0-669-03305-7

Library of Congress Catalog Card Number: 79-2978

Contents

Foreword

William Prast has written a remarkably succinct book about a timely and urgent topic: how to secure the energy supplies needed for America's future.

Prast's account is a clear and sane voice in the confused and proliferating babble of partisanship, recrimination, and fantasy that has come to dominate much of the market of energy ideas. "Hyperbolic language," he rightly warns, "is of no value in making balanced decisions." His own language is calm and modest, and the solutions he suggests are many-sided and encompassing.

There is need for private initiative as well as public regulation as we solve our energy problems. We cannot relapse into the "primrose mentality regarding energy supply and suppliers"—the naive optimism of the 1960s, which left us so utterly unprepared for the international oil shocks of the 1970s. Much of the job of finding new energy supplies will continue to have to be done by the private sector. But we must keep asking, as does Dr. Prast, "how well these private companies are meeting public goals." Since so many of our reserves of natural gas, coal, and uranium are on federal land, a new type of public or private-public company may prove to be a desirable ingredient in our future policy. Among other benefits, it might raise the level of expertise and competence in the growing federal energy bureaucracy.

To allow domestic energy prices to rise to internationally set levels, as we now are committed to doing, is a simple act of prudence and realism—valuing the energy we consume at its true replacement cost. But price deregulation will not result in any instant cornucopia of new supplies—we would disregard technological lead times at our peril.

The book's opening chapter, with a few deft strokes, manages to convey to the reader a sound statistical picture of our present pattern of energy production and consumption. After many years when environmentalists and energy specialists seem to have done more shouting at than listening to each other, it is refreshing to come across Dr. Prast's simple insistence that environmental factors will have to be an integral part of all future energy calculations. There also are obvious possibilities for conservation—but, as the author strikingly puts it, conservation is no more than "the collateral against which more energy-adjustment time is borrowed." The adjustment itself will have to rely on a combination of all the sources available, including coal, oil, gas, nuclear, some synthetic fuels, and a growing variety of solar resources.

As we develop such balanced programs for the future, we must avoid the "proclivity to crisis management" that has marred so many of our efforts of the past decade. As Dr. Prast reminds us, the United States was a net energy exporter as recently as 1957; and today we are still self-sufficient for as much as 81 percent of our energy consumption. *Securing U.S. Energy Supplies* is a sound guide through the available solutions as we cope with the remaining 19 percent of the problem.

Dankwart A. Rustow
Distinguished Professor of Political Science
City University, Graduate School

Preface and Acknowledgments

The search for satisfactory public-policy alternatives to reduce American dependence on imported petroleum has called into question the role of private energy-producing companies in executing these policies. Historically the task of securing the energy supplies of the United States was a matter of concern only to the firms involved, but this state of affairs is no longer tolerable in a period of relatively higher energy costs and supply uncertainties.

This book identifies some of the policy options that are open for using the private companies as constructive instruments of energy supply. It points out certain conflicts and inherent tensions between these companies and the public agencies that control their activities, concentrating upon the changing role of the federal government. My purpose is not to provide pat answers to energy policymakers or their advisers but rather to stimulate discussion and consideration of certain public choices.

Numerous people deserve mention for their contributions to the production of this work, including many persons who have been part of my twenty years of experience in the energy industry. For their many hours of creative thinking and articulate debate on energy-policy issues, particular thanks must be given to J. Alan Cope and Robert M. Heine, former colleagues at Conoco Inc. Research assistance was provided by several members of Atlantis Energy and Mineral Economic Services, Inc., including Rudi P. Fronk and J.R. Martin. Important improvements to the text were suggested by Thomas R. Berkel and Howard L. Lax, who acted as constructively critical editors. Typing services were provided by Joan Starr, and indexing was done by Anne Meagher. The project would never have begun, and would certainly not have been completed, without the enduring patience and encouragement of my wife, Barbara Jane, who provided all manner of support throughout the venture.

All errors of fact and misconceptions of opinion are solely mine and are acknowledged in advance of their being pointed out by readers.

Securing U.S. Energy Supplies

1 Perspective: U.S. Energy Supply and Demand

The United States has built its economy upon ready access to large quantities of inexpensive energy, and consequently the achievement of secure energy supplies has been a key public-policy goal. For most of the twentieth century, America was a net energy exporter, but that status has changed, and in the case of oil in particular, the country is now dependent on imports. The private sector historically has been the principal instrument for finding and developing the sources of American energy, here and abroad, but its role for the future has been under question in recent years. Critics and apologists of the large, private, energy companies often have resorted to strident language in an effort to convince the general public of their views. It is clear that hyperbolic language is of no value in making balanced decisions, but the headlines often emphasize the more extreme viewpoints that are put forward in order to influence public opinion.

This book seeks to describe the role of the private sector as an instrument of public policy striving to achieve U.S. energy-supply goals, with special emphasis upon policy options that may be exercised in order to acquire the secure supplies of low-cost energies that the nation requires.

Energy Consumption Patterns

The United States has been the largest consumer of energy in the world for many years. Although its relative share of global energy consumption is declining slowly, it still accounts for some 30 percent of annual overall consumption. Currently the Department of Energy reports that the United States is consuming approximately 75 quadrillion Btu per annum, with world consumption running about 250 quadrillion Btu per annum. In comparison to American energy demand, annual consumption of all forms of energy in Western Europe is approximately 50 quadrillion Btu, in Japan 15 quadrillion Btu, and in the rest of the world a combined 110 quadrillion Btu.

The massive appetite for energy in the United States reflects the size of the gross national product (GNP). When American energy demand is measured in terms of the quantity of energy required per dollar of GNP, it is clear that there has been a slow decrease in the energy consumption per dollar of GNP during the postwar period. Data issued by the Department of Energy and by the American Petroleum Institute indicate that, whereas in 1947, 70,500 Btu of gross energy input was required per dollar of GNP (measured in terms of 1972 dollars), this input has declined to approximately 58,000 Btu per 1972 dollar of GNP at the present time.

Measured in terms of gross energy consumption per capita, the input of energy rose sharply from a 1947 level of 229 million Btu per capita to a postwar peak of 354 million Btu per capita in 1973. Following the Arab oil embargo in the autumn of 1973, there was a slight downward adjustment in energy consumption during the recession that followed, with a modest drop to 345 million Btu per capita in 1976, and a slow rise since then, according to the Department of the Interior statistical series.

The largest single sources of energy are petroleum and natural gas. Over 45 percent of the gross national energy input is petroleum based, with natural gas providing an additional 22 percent of the American energy base. Petroleum consumption amounts to some 7.5 billion barrels per year. Half of this amount is consumed as transportation fuels, principally as motor gasoline, diesel fuel, and aviation jet kerosene. Approximately one-fifth is used in each of the household-commercial and industrial sectors. American consumption of natural gas is approximately 20 trillion cubic feet per annum, of which industrial uses account for almost half, and household-commercial applications, principally space heating, account for another 40 percent, reports the American Petroleum Institute. Unlike petroleum, which is imported to the extent of almost half of domestic demand, there is relatively little imported natural gas, other than some overland shipments from Canada and tanker shipments of liquefied natural gas.

Coal accounts for approximately 18 percent of American gross energy inputs. About half of all electricity generated in the United States is derived from coal, and electric utilities account for about 70 percent of the coal burned in this country. Other energy sources that yield only electricity include nuclear power, which provides approximately 4 percent of gross energy inputs, and hydropower and geothermal sources, which provide an additional 6 percent, according to the U.S. Bureau of Mines studies. In terms of physical units, coal consumption is about 700 million tons per annum, all of it derived from domestic sources. Nuclear power currently is generating approximately 400 billion kilowatt hours per annum, and hydro and geothermal electricity sources are contributing 350 billion kilowatt hours per annum.

Changing Market Shares

During the postwar years, the position of coal has declined from that of the primary fuel source to third rank, behind petroleum and natural gas.

As recently as 1949, coal contributed 40 percent of American gross energy consumption, but its share of domestic energy inputs is now barely 18 percent. Petroleum, on the other hand, has retained its share of some 48 percent of total energy consumption for years. Its share of U.S. total gross consumption of energy has been above 40 percent since 1951, generally around 45 percent since the mid-1950s.

Natural-gas consumption, which was less than one-seventh of American gross energy consumption in 1947, reached 25 percent in 1957 and exceeded 30 percent for the first time in 1963. After peaking at one-third of total energy consumption in 1971, natural-gas output began to decrease, and the relative proportion of U.S. energy supplies from that source has receded to approximately one-quarter of national fuels consumption.

Hydropower, converted to theoretical energy inputs calculated from national average heat rates for fossil-fuel steam electric plants, has generated 4 percent of total gross energy since the 1950s. A steady growth in hydroelectric power has permitted this energy source to hold its relative position, although most of the promising hydropower sites have now been developed.

Nuclear power, which first came into commercial production in 1957, has experienced a hectic twenty years of growth. Nuclear power contributed 3.9 percent of U.S. total gross consumption of energy in 1978, the equivalent of some 3 trillion Btu, reports the Department of Energy "Monthly Energy Review." Despite considerable public uncertainty about the safety and security aspects of nuclear power, the probability of its continuing to provide base-load electricity, in line with its current contribution, seems high. With all nuclear power going into electricity production, it accounts for approximately 13 percent of all U.S. electricity generation.

Domestic Sources and Imports

Although the United States imports half of its petroleum requirements, a widely publicized fact, it is less well known that the country is self-sufficient for approximately 81 percent of its total gross energy consumption. Coal, oil, and natural gas are well balanced as the three leading domestic sources. In the most recent year for which data are available, 1976, the production of 15.8 quadrillion Btu of coal accounted for 26.4 percent of U.S. domestic production of energy resources. U.S.-based petroleum output of 17.2 quadrillion Btu accounted for 28.8 percent, and natural gas (21.8 quadrillion Btu) accounted for 36.4 percent. The remainder comprised 3.0 trillion Btu of hydropower (5.0 percent) and 2.0 quadrillion Btu of nuclear power (3.4 percent). Thus total domestic gross energy inputs were 59.8 quadrillion Btu, as against a total domestic gross energy consumption of 74.0 quadrillion Btu. The difference was made up mostly by oil imports.

Although the United States domestically produces four-fifths of its gross energy consumption, this is the lowest percentage in history. As recently as 1957, the United States was a net exporter of energy. Not until 1971 did the United States fall below a 90 percent self-sufficiency in energy production, a decrease almost exclusively attributable to the rise of petroleum imports used in the transportation-fuels sector and to meet consumer preferences for petroleum over coal as a fuel to heat buildings.

The future position of the United States regarding energy self-sufficiency is unclear. Certainly the country can expand its coal production beyond the present 700 million tons per annum. The future role of coal will grow relatively more quickly if reliance on an electricity-based economy continues to develop and if the use of coal for the generation of synthetic petroleum and synthetic natural gas evolves. It is less likely that the United States can sustain its current annual production of some 3 billion barrels of petroleum and 20 trillion cubic feet of natural gas from domestic sources. Assuming that hydroelectric power does not grow much beyond its present level of 300 billion kilowatt hours per annum and that nuclear power remains stalemated because of environmental and health concerns at an equivalency of approximately 200 billion kilowatt hours per annum, there will continue to be a need to reexamine the primary fuel source mix very carefully and to consider our fuel options closely. Lead times to develop alternatives are quite long, measured in decades for many energy-supply projects.

Uses of Energy

All energy is consumed in order to achieve other purposes. Gross energy is that contained in all types of commercial energy at the time it is incorporated in the economy, whether the energy is produced domestically or is imported. Gross energy includes inputs of primary fuel or their derivatives, and outputs of hydropower and nuclear power converted to theoretical energy inputs. Gross energy also includes that energy that is required to produce, process, and transport energy power.

Household and commercial applications take approximately 15 quadrillion Btu, or one-fifth of U.S. gross consumption of energy. Industrial applications require an additional 18 quadrillion Btu, or 25 percent, with transportation also absorbing approximately 25 percent of total energy consumed. Electricity generation accounts for the remaining 30 percent.

The distribution of U.S. gross energy consumption by consuming sector has shifted gradually. Since the 1950s, the fraction consumed in the household and commercial sector has fluctuated around 20 percent, but the amount required for industrial output has decreased slowly. In 1950, over 36 percent of U.S. gross energy consumption was for industrial purposes, but this amount dropped below 30 percent after 1970 and has now reached 25 percent. The transportation sector has remained almost unchanged at 25 percent of gross energy consumption for three decades.

The electricity-generating sector has shown the most growth, effectively doubling its share of gross energy consumption since the 1950s. In 1948 electricity generation accounted for less than one-seventh of U.S. gross energy consumption. This fraction reached one-fifth in 1964 and exceeded one-quarter for the first time in 1971. Currently it is approaching 30 percent of U.S. gross consumption of energy, indicating how electrification of the economy has become a major feature of the national energy scene.

A sectorial analysis indicates how the bituminous-coal industry has altered its mix of end uses, after undergoing a period of retrenchment prior to the present growth phase, to spur a record level of production. The almost complete elimination of the household and commercial sector and the rail transportation sector as markets for coal has been offset by the rise in the use of coal to generate electricity. Thirty years ago, less than 100 million tons of coal per annum were burned in power plants. This fuel use now accounts each year for more than 450 million tons of coal; over 70 percent of U.S. coal burned in the United States is to make electricity.

The demand for natural gas, on the other hand, has shown a steady growth in the household and commercial sectors, as well as the industrial sector. Approximately 8 trillion cubic feet of gas are used for space-heating purposes in the household and commercial sector, double the level of 1959 and more than eight times that of 1947. Industrial use of natural gas peaked at slightly less than 10 trillion cubic feet per annum in 1973 and is now declining, with present consumption rates of 7 trillion cubic feet per year.

In electrical generation, too, natural gas seems to have reached its high point. In 1971 4 trillion cubic feet were burned to generate electricity, but the amount of gas used today for that purpose is below 3 trillion cubic feet per annum. The decline will continue because of federal legislation, the 1978 Power Plant and Industrial Fuel Use Act, prohibiting the use of oil or natural gas as a fuel in new electric-power plants.

The petroleum sector has enjoyed a very balanced distribution of demand. Consumption for transportation uses has doubled since 1947, currently accounting for about 3.5 billion barrels of oil per annum. Household and commercial use has risen modestly and remains under 1 billion barrels per annum, a quantity that is approximately the same as that in 1970, according to the U.S. Department of the Interior. In the industrial sector, growth has been steady but unspectacular, approaching 700 million barrels per annum, up from 450 million barrels in 1955.

The use of oil for electricity generation reached 500 million barrels in 1972 and has remained at that rate. Probably it will decline as utilities substitute coal for oil as a boiler fuel in the future. The period of rapid growth in electricity generation was between 1964 and 1972, when demand rose from 100 million barrels to 500 million barrels per annum.

Prospects for Change

The shape of the American economy prevents any short-term permanent shifts in the energy-use pattern. The replacement of fuel-burning facilities requires substantial investment in new capital equipment, and lead times of many years are required to purchase and install this equipment. Thus, it is improbable that any short-term shifts can be large. On the other hand, it is possible to identify the direction in which American energy supply and consumption is likely to proceed.

Despite efforts to reduce the present reliance upon imports, it must be anticipated that foreign countries will continue to be significant sources of U.S. energy supplies for some years to come. Because approximately 75 percent of total fuel use is derived from petroleum and natural gas, any transition away from these fuels, either domestic or imported, will take many years. During the period of transition, it is important that public policies reflect the need to ensure supplies of these materials, while at the same time encouraging a steady movement toward alternatives that could provide more-secure and less-costly fuels.

Considerable uncertainty over the outlook for public acceptance of atomic power makes it very difficult to anticipate the role that this fuel may play in generating electricity during the balance of the century. The lead times required for the installation of new nuclear generators are about ten years, substantially longer than was the case fifteen years ago when less-elaborate safeguard and review procedures were required.

The reluctant shift toward more coal use that is now beginning could prove to be an ironic boost to atomic power. The possibility cannot be ruled out that any significant growth in the direct burning of coal could bring about a reaction against this fuel source on environmental grounds that might more than equal the public anxiety concerning nuclear power. Although there are many valid reasons why coal might be promoted as a substitute for nuclear or other fuels, offsetting factors have thwarted bituminous coal from seizing this opportunity. In addition to the environmental constraints that curtail the mining of coal, severe capital-cost handicaps need to be overcome by the electric utilities. Expensive new equipment is required to clean up the flue gas from the smoke stacks, and numerous environmental health and safety regulations add costs during the process of mining and preparing the coal. Despite the rapid deterioration in the economic attractiveness of nuclear power, as a result of cost escalations and extensions of the timetables necessary to install new atomic-generating equipment, the cost disadvantage of coal as an electric-utility fuel has not been overcome.

Labor-relations problems in the American coal fields are yet another deterrent to the rapid growth in coal output. Historically the United Mine Workers of America has mounted substantial strikes at three-year intervals, when contracts expire, and there have been extensive periodic and irregular strikes throughout the life of the contract. These wildcat strikes stem from the ambitions and militancy of miners who see their role in supplying American energy supplies as increasingly important to society.

Over the long term, it should be possible for the United States to use its coal base and its oil-related resources such as tar sands and oil shale to generate fuels that satisfy consumer demand patterns. Coal, oil shale, and tar sands can produce liquid hydrocarbons and synthetic gas, which can be mixed with natural gas in the existing pipeline network. A gradual development of these synthetic fuels would require an unprecedented cooperation between the federal government and the private sector to ensure that the technology and capital required are brought to bear in a timely fashion with an acceptable social and economic benefit for all concerned. Various funding techniques to achieve this goal have been suggested, but none have been agreed upon as yet.

Longer-Term Outlook

In addition to the prospects for a steady expansion in the use of coal and other nonpetroleum hydrocarbon sources, there are growing prospects for an eventual shift toward renewable energy resources. Although advocates for the use of solar power and alternative renewable power sources have demanded a rapid transition to these sources, partially as a social and political reaction to the alleged abuses of the energy companies, electric utilities, and other large institutions, it is not probable that a quick shift could be engineered. The massive capital costs and industrial dislocations to the economy of a quick move are not likely to be affordable unless a major crisis requires such action. But despite the unlikely short-term prospects for major contributions being made by these energy resources, there are many prospects for spurring their selective use. The accumulative effect of their introduction in a variety of applications could be helpful, and all methods for substituting imported petroleum warrant careful attention.

In the American political system, the general public always exercises some influence over the decision-making processes that largely shape energy policies. In their various roles as consumers, voters, interest-group members, and constituent parts in that amorphous variable known as public opinion, the people play both direct and indirect roles in influencing energy decisions. Moreover, these influences affect decision makers at various levels; individual firms, elected officials (both state and federal), and the relevant bureaucracies all are affected, to some extent, by the public. A number of examples indicate the influence that the public has on American energy policies: the de facto moratorium on the construction of new nuclear reactors in the United States in the wake of the 1979 accident at Three Mile Island and the slow growth that the atomic power industry experienced prior to that incident; court actions instituted by public-interest and consumer groups bottlenecking numerous energy exploration and development programs on environmental and health grounds; regional and interstate disputes over energy shipments and prices between energy-producing and energy-importing states; and plebiscites on nuclear energy held in California and other states.

A central factor in evaluating the contribution of the public in defining U.S. policy during times of energy scarcity and uncertainty is the quality of public participation. A greater awareness of energy facts and policy options should enable citizens to act prudently and reasonably with respect to important energy-related decisions. The demands of democracy would ideally be satisfied by the active participation of an educated electorate and citizenry.

The public, however, rarely performs according to the theoretical standards of enlightened, rational participation in the political processes. Improving the quality of the public debate about and general understanding of energy issues, and thereby promoting the democratic influence of the people, should be a goal of the government. Only through the fostering of such an improved public understanding can popular consensus with respect to energy make a positive contribution to the decision-making processes and help steer the country away from the danger of an energy-policy failure. Even if a lively, well-educated public debate began, the changeable nature of public opinion, being prey to anxiety, sensationalism, and short-term influences, could offset the healthy influence of responsible efforts at education and discussion.

Traditionally American decision makers respond to issues as they arise. The absence of an institutionalized process of long-term planning and the concomitant tendency to resort to reliance upon ad hoc decision making to address specific short-term problems is reinforced by a public that shows an interest in issues only when they have a direct bearing upon their lives. The result is a process often referred to as crisis management. The proclivity for crisis management means that American energy policy tends to be the by-product of a series of disjointed reactions to periodic problems rather than the product of the rational formulation of strategies in anticipation of long-term concerns. The results are uncoordinated policies and incremental decision making that are usually too parochial and of too limited a time frame to provide any guidance for future policy or to take into account the consequences of its own actions. The absence of a well-entrenched energy bureaucracy and the historical complacency of the United States with respect to energy matters have lent further impetus to crisis management as the means of identifying and formulating public energy goals.

The habitual tendency of the United States to make policy adjustments through crisis-period decisions encourages the technique of muddling through. Although it is understandable that the public displays only a minimal interest in energy during times when there are no shortages, for decision making to be effective there must be a continuous process of innovation. Effective policy making necessitates the use of a time frame whose horizon extends beyond imminent issues.

There are no simple solutions for achieving an agreement on the most-desirable energy policy and supply mix that best satisfy public requirements. A gradual transition from the present unsatisfactory balance of energy supplies to a healthier mix of energy sources in the coming decade demands a cooperative effort among the various levels of government, existing energy suppliers, and the general public within the framework of a national consensus on American energy-policy goals and strategies. Such a consensus, however, cannot emerge from crisis-management decisions but it can develop from institutionalized processes of continuous decision making and policy evaluation in anticipation of, rather than in response to, the inevitable crises and concerns that beset all countries in their efforts to formulate effective energy policies.

2 Organization of U.S. Energy Supplies

The production and delivery of energy require ownership of an energy reserve. These processes involve numerous companies, ranging from huge integrated international corporations to firms of very modest size. Within the U.S. fuels industry, the scale and organization of the firms varies according to the type of fuel. Some corporations are engaged in producing more than one energy source, notably those companies that began in oil and gas and grew through horizontal integration into coal or uranium.

Oil and Gas

Reserves

The holdings of proven U.S. crude-oil condensate and natural-gas liquid reserves are slightly concentrated, with the eight largest organizations controlling slightly more than 55 percent of these total proven reserves, according to reports by the American Petroleum Institute.

There are more than ten thousand oil- and gas-exploration and production companies in the United States. Although 80 percent of proven petroleum reserves are held by fewer than forty companies, the balance of these reserves is divided among many firms. Because of its substantial holdings of Alaskan North Slope petroleum, the company with the largest holding of U.S. crude-oil reserves is Standard Oil of Ohio (Sohio). Its reserves total 4.4 billion barrels, over 12 percent of total proven reserves. Eight other companies have reserves in excess of 1 billion barrels (each 1 billion barrels represents more than 3 percent of total U.S. reserves): Exxon, Arco, Texaco, Amoco, Shell, Getty, Chevron, and Gulf.

The pattern of holdings of proven reserves of natural gas shows slightly less concentration. The eight largest companies own less than 40 percent of natural-gas reserves, and the forty largest firms hold under 70 percent of reserves. Ranked first in natural-gas-reserves ownership is Exxon, whose reserves of 19.5 trillion cubic feet represent a bit more than 9 percent of total U.S. reserves. The other leading firms are Texaco, Arco, Amoco, Mobil, Shell, Sohio, and Gulf.

11

Pipeline and distribution companies, which have specialized in the production and sale of natural gas, feature prominently in natural-gas-reserve holdings. Their acquisition of gas by purchase of reserves or through their own exploration effort has resulted in the development of such firms as El Paso, Consolidated Natural Gas, Panhandle Eastern Coastal States, and the Columbia Gas system. All have acquired more than 1 trillion cubic feet of the 200 trillion feet of proven natural-gas reserves in the United States.

Production

Not surprisingly, there is a close relationship between the production of oil and gas and the control of reserves. In the United States, daily production of crude oil, condensate, and natural-gas liquids is about 9.8 million barrels per day, with the top eight firms producing almost 40 percent of this amount. Leading the group is Exxon, with daily production of almost 800,000 barrels per day, or 8 percent of the national total. The other top eight firms are Texaco, Shell, Amoco, Arco, Gulf, Chevron, and Mobil, each of which contributes more than 3 percent of total U.S. petroleum production.

The top forty firms produce slightly less than two-thirds of U.S. crude oil, with the remaining one-third of the oil output distributed among several thousand other firms. Among these forty largest oil producers are firms whose parent companies are not noted as energy companies. For example, Champlin, whose production is above 50,000 barrels per day, is owned by the Union Pacific Corporation; Aminoil, with a comparable production, is owned by R.J. Reynolds; and General Crude Oil was owned by International Paper until 1979.

The concentration in the ownership of U.S. crude oil production has risen slightly in recent years. The twenty largest oil-producing firms lift almost 6 million barrels per day, or nearly 60 percent of the national total. This reflects a decrease from the peak years in the early 1970s when the twenty largest firms produced more than 62 percent of U.S. oil. This degree of concentration, reached during the 1972–1974 period, was preceded by almost twenty years of growth from 46 percent for the top twenty firms in 1955.

U.S. net natural-gas production of 20 billion cubic feet is supplied by several thousand companies, of which the top forty firms produce 60 percent. Leading the group is Exxon, whose output is 1.5 trillion cubic feet, or 7.6 percent of U.S. total production. Following Exxon are many of the same large oil companies who hold natural-gas reserves. As in the case of oil, there has been a slight decrease in the degree of concentration of natural-gas production held by the leading companies. The top twenty firms produce over 10 trillion cubic feet, or 52 percent of total U.S. production. This same group of twenty firms produced as much as 58 percent in 1970, up from liftings of less than 50 percent during the 1950s.

Refining

Because of the vertically integrated nature of the oil industry, U.S. refining-capacity holdings show many of the same firms already identified as major owners and producers of petroleum. U.S. refining capacity is over 17 million barrels per day, and there are about 250 refineries in the United States. Approximately 78 percent (or 13.3 million barrels per day) is controlled by the top twenty firms, and the top forty firms hold more than 90 percent of American refining capacity. The balance of 10 percent is scattered among numerous small refining companies, which have taken advantage of federal legislation to construct very small refineries and thus receive special entitlement provisions provided by federal law. These entitlements have enabled very small companies to be profit-making operations despite their otherwise uneconomically small size. The largest of the U.S. refiners is Exxon, with 1.6 million barrels per day of refining capacity, almost 9 percent of the national total. Chevron, Amoco, Shell, and Texaco also own refining capacity in excess of 1 million barrels per day apiece.

The American Petroleum Institute indicates that the portion of U.S. refining capacity controlled by the top twenty firms has remained around 80 percent, plus or minus 4 percentage points, since 1950. The capital-intensive nature of petroleum refining has resulted in relatively few changes in these league tables over time. Exxon has been the leading U.S. refiner for the past thirty years. The second position, now held by Chevron, has been held by Shell and Amoco on different occasions during the 1970s.

Pipelines

Interstate oil pipelines are the primary means of transporting petroleum products and crude oil in bulk within the United States. Pipeline trunkline capacity is measured in terms of barrel miles, an indication of the carrying capacity measured in terms of the size and length of the line. The twenty biggest interstate pipeline firms control 85 percent, or 2.8 million barrel-miles, of capacity; the total U.S. trunkline capacity is 3.3 million barrel miles.

Ranked first according to the American Petroleum Institute is Amoco, with 294,000 barrel miles (9 percent), followed by Texaco, Gulf,

Exxon, Shell, and Mobil, all with more than 5 percent of the overall interstate oil pipeline capacity. The share of pipeline capacity held by the largest companies has been dropping, however. Whereas the top eight firms held 71 percent of the barrel-miles capacity in 1951, the expansion of the national pipeline grid through investments by newcomers has caused this share to fall to about 50 percent currently.

Petroleum Marketing

Although marketing is but one step in the chain of oil-industry activities, it is the aspect that is most familiar to the general public. U.S. refined-products sales, averaging 18.5 million barrels per day, involve the participation of several thousand companies. The top twenty marketing firms supply 77 percent of the market according to the American Petroleum Institute and are led by Exxon, whose 1.7 million barrels per day of refined-products sales represents 9.5 percent of total sales. The second largest petroleum marketer, Amoco, sells 1.3 million barrels per day, or 7 percent of the national demand, followed closely by Texaco and Chevron. Shell, the fifth largest marketer with a 5.6 percent share, also sells in excess of 1 million barrels per day. The market control of the top twenty firms has been slipping, however. In 1965, these firms supplied over 86 percent of the national market. This dominance has diminished and is now under 78 percent.

   Gasoline, the largest component of U.S. petroleum demand, warrants separate consideration. U.S. sales of motor gasoline exceed 100 billion gallons annually, with the twenty largest firms selling over 70 percent, or about 80 billion gallons. Ranked first is Shell, with aggregate motor gasolines sales of 8.4 billion gallons (7.6 percent of the total market). Following Shell, with similar market shares of 7.1 percent and sales of 8.0 billion barrels, are Amoco, Exxon, and Texaco. Gulf, with 6.6 billion gallons (6 percent of the market) and Mobil with 6.2 billion gallons of sales (5.6 percent) round out the top half-dozen.

   For a number of years prior to 1977, Texaco had been the nation's leading gasoline marketer, with sales in every state. In 1977 Texaco fell from its perennial first position to the fourth-place slot because of a policy decision to cut back on the unprofitable retailing of motor gasoline and withdraw from certain states.

Coal

A different pattern of ownership and supply is apparent in other energy sectors. The coal industry, with reserves accounting for 90 percent of all

U.S. energy reserves, includes a variety of companies whose requirements for coal have encouraged them to develop captive sources. Included in this group are steel companies and electric utilities, which have integrated vertically into coal ownership and production to meet their own needs.

The U.S. Geological Survey estimates that the total U.S. coal-reserve base suitable for economic mining by current methods is 434 billion tons. Allowing for a recovery rate of 50 percent for underground mining and 80 percent for surface mining, the estimated recoverable reserves are approximately 250 billion tons.

No one company holds as much as 6 percent of total U.S. reserves of coal. Most U.S. coal is located on publicly owned lands in the western states, and the federal government is custodian of more coal than anyone else. Among private companies, the firm with the largest coal-reserve holdings is Consolidation Coal, a subsidiary of Conoco Inc. Consolidation Coal reports coal reserves of 13.7 billion tons, or slightly more than 5 percent of the U.S. recoverable reserves.

Next in order of reserve holding is Peabody Coal Company, which was affiliated with Kennecott for some years. Peabody was subject to a divestiture order by the Federal Trade Commission, and in June 1977 Kennecott sold its coal holdings to a consortium, Peabody Holding Company, owned by Newmont Mining (27.5 percent), the Williams Companies (27.5 percent), Bechtel (15 percent), Boeing (15 percent), Fluor (10 percent), and the Equitable Life Assurance Society (5 percent).

The Exxon coal subsidiary, Monterrey Coal, ranks third in total coal-reserves holdings, with 8.4 billion tons, or slightly more than 3 percent of the national total. Four other firms reporting holdings of more than 5 billion tons of coal reserves are the Burlington Northern railroad, with coal lands acquired in the mid-nineteenth century; El Paso Natural Gas; the independent North American Coal; and Amax Coal, a subsidiary of the large metal-mining company, which in turn is 21 percent owned by Standard Oil of California (Chevron). Rounding out the top ten are Island Creek, a subsidiary of Occidental Petroleum, Mobil, and the United States Steel Corporation.

Oil firms in aggregate hold more than 56 million tons (23 percent) of U.S. coal. There are approximately twenty-five oil-related companies with coal holdings, including such firms as Rocky Mountain Energy, a subsidiary of the Union Pacific Corporation.

The absence of concentration in coal holdings is attributable to the ease of entry into the industry and the general abundance of coal. It is relatively simple for would-be coal-mining firms to acquire acreage with commercial reserves and to master the relatively simple technology for surface mining. Consequently the twenty-firm concentration ratio for coal-reserves ownership shows holdings of 82 billion tons, or less than one-third of national reserves.

Coal ownership alone is no indication of productive capacity, however. Many firms hold large amounts of coal that are not being offered on the market, others are developing reserves, and others have coal in surplus of their immediate requirements.

American coal production is in excess of 700 million tons per annum. Since approximately 1975, the largest coal producer has been Peabody, whose annual market share is around 10 percent of U.S. output. Second to Peabody is Consolidation Coal, with some 6 to 8 percent of national production. Amax Coal is the third largest coal producer, with 28 million tons (4 percent). Following Amax, in order, are Island Creek, the Occidental subsidiary; Pitston Company, an independent firm; and the captive coal mines of U.S. Steel. Nearly all of the U.S. Steel coal production is for metallurgical-grade coking coal. Rounding out the top ten producers are Arch Minerals, a 50-percent-owned affiliate of Ashland Oil; Nerco, the coal-supply arm of Pacific Power and Light; and Bethlehem Steel Corporation's affiliate, Bethlehem Mines Corporation; and Peter Kiewit & Sons, a construction company that entered surface mining and now operates one of the largest open-pit coal mines in the United States.

The top eight producing firms lift some 31 percent of all U.S. coal or 210 million tons. The top twenty firms produced 314 million tons or 46 percent of the national total. The highly fragmented nature of American coal mining is further demonstrated by the fact that the top forty coal companies represent less than 60 percent of the national output.

The production of bituminous coal from consumer owned or so-called captive mines has now reached more than 100 million tons per annum, and represents some 16 percent of all U.S. bituminous coal production. Approximately one-half of this segment is held by American steel producers, with most of the remaining 50 percent in the hands of various electric utilities. Prior to the demise of coal as a transportation fuel, railroads were also a significant direct factor in the coal mining industry.

According to data from the National Coal Association, there are more than 6,000 active coal mines in the United States. Sixty percent or some thirty-seven hundred of these are surface mines, and about twenty-four hundred are underground mines. Coal is produced in twenty-six states. Kentucky ranks first, providing more than 140 million tons per annum. Following Kentucky in the ranking are West Virginia with annual production on the order of 100 million tons, Pennsylvania (80 million tons), Illinois, and Ohio.

Mining techniques vary widely among regions. In Appalachia, the bulk of coal is produced from underground mines; in the western states, surface mining predominates. For example, in West Virginia more than three-quarters of coal output is from underground mines. At the other extreme, Wyoming produces more than 40 million tons per annum, all of it from surface mines.

Uranium

U.S. uranium-oxide reserves are reported by the Department of Energy in terms of their forward costs, a measure of the cost of production exclusive of taxes, profit margins, and certain other expenditures. The concept is not a market-price one. Based upon the forward-cost estimate method, U.S. total reserves of uranium oxide available at under $15 per pound are some 370,000 tons. One company, Kerr-McGee, controls 145,000 tons, or almost two-fifths of total U.S. reserves. Kerr-McGee is also a minor factor in the oil industry, producing 0.5 percent of U.S. petroleum and natural gas.

Unlike the coal industry, metal-mining and oil firms dominate the American uranium industry, and ownership of uranium-reserves holdings is more concentrated. Other leading holders of uranium reserves include Gulf, United Nuclear, an independent company, Conoco Inc., Phelps Dodge, Exxon, Getty, and Arco (which owns Anaconda). The top eight uranium reserve holders, based on the $15 cutoff level, control more than 93 percent of this reserve.

Because the average price of uranium now is about $30 per pound, it is more meaningful to consider the total reserve estimate based on $30 per pound forward costs. Using this yardstick, the top eight firms hold less than 50 percent of American uranium reserves. And as one increases the reserve estimate to $50 per pound, the share held by the top eight firms drops to under 39 percent.

Insofar as the production of uranium-oxide concentrate is concerned, the top eight firms represent slightly more than 55 percent of American output, about 17,000 tons per annum. The leader is Kerr-McGee, with more than 13 percent of total U.S. production, or 2,300 tons per annum. Anaconda ranks second and United Nuclear third, with Exxon and the British-controlled Rio Algom ranking fourth and fifth, respectively. Other uranium producers in the top ten include the Phelps Dodge–affiliate Western Nuclear, Commonwealth Edison of Illinois, Conoco, Amax, and Sohio. Oil companies, including Kerr-McGee, Exxon, Conoco, Sohio, Gulf and Arco, produce more than 6,000 tons of uranium oxide, or 37 percent of the national output.

More than 150 firms are now engaged in uranium exploration, but the bulk of production is still accomplished by thirty or forty companies, which have their ore processed by some eighteen mills throughout the country. The production of uranium and its fabrication into fuel rods for the nuclear-power industry is strongly influenced by the federal government, dating back to the period before commercial nuclear reactors were initiated in the late 1950s. The enrichment process, by which uranium oxide is converted into uranium hexafluoride, is a government monopoly carried out at three enrichment plants under the auspices of the Department of Energy.

Energy Supplies by Firms

Perhaps the most instructive way to look at American energy supply is in terms of the concentration levels for oil, natural gas, coal, and uranium combined in terms of Btu and dollar value. Considering first the U.S. energy-producing companies on a Btu basis, Exxon produces 6 percent of total U.S. energy according to American Petroleum Institute estimates. In 1977, a recent typical year, some 62 quadrillion Btu of energy was generated from all sources in the United States, and Exxon contributed 3.7 quadrillion Btu. Following Exxon in terms of aggregate energy production were Texaco, Arco, Amoco, Conoco, Shell, Gulf, and Peabody. These top eight firms generated 17.3 quadrillion Btu, or 28 percent of all U.S. energy production. The percentage of total domestic energy that is supplied by Exxon fell slightly in the 1970s but nevertheless doubled since 1960. In 1960, Exxon (then the Standard Oil Company of New Jersey) produced 1.5 quadrillion Btu of the 48 quadrillion Btu produced in the United States, or 3.1 percent of total energy production.

Viewed in terms of the dollar value of the energy produced, the pattern is not dissimilar. Again Exxon ranks first with $3.7 billion, or 6.1 percent of total U.S. energy production, valued at $60 billion in 1977. Texaco was second, with Amoco ranking third, Shell fourth, and Gulf fifth, but Arco and Conoco slipped lower because of the lower dollar value of a Btu of coal. The top eight firms yielded 30 percent by value of U.S. energy production in 1977, or $17.8 billion in aggregate. The top twenty-five firms, all of which except Peabody are considered as primarily oil companies, generated $25.7 billion, or 42.7 percent of total U.S. energy production in 1977.

The share by value of U.S. energy production that is contributed by the leading eight firms, 30 percent, has been in the range of 25 to 35 percent since the mid-1950s. Some critics are anxious that there should not be growth in this degree of concentration and believe that the existing levels of concentration already may be excessive.

3 Integrated Energy Firms

American society is extraordinarily energy intensive. Annual U.S. gross consumption of energy is about 75 quadrillion Btu, the equivalent of sixty barrels of oil per person per annum. Most Americans are aware of their energy consumption only in terms of those uses that they control directly, that is, they think in terms of their needs for gasoline, domestic heating, and lighting. But these perceptions are incomplete. Transportation fuels, for example, account for only 26 percent of U.S. energy consumption, and electricity is derived from primary sources of energy such as coal, fossil fuels, or water power. Thus to understand the organization of American energy supply, it is necessary to look beyond the gasoline station sign or the name on the home-heating oil truck and examine the structure of those firms that provide national energy needs. Energy-producing companies have widely varying activities. Some variations have resulted from the history of individual firms, but generally the organization of energy companies has evolved in response to the economics of the fuels industries and to the political regulations controlling their investment alternatives.

Petroleum Industry

Vertical Integration

The wide range of activities pursued by the larger oil and gas corporations indicates that they find economic advantages in being integrated. In this context, vertical integration refers to the extension of business from one part of an industry, such as exploration for crude oil and natural gas, into allied sectors, such as the production of petroleum. Full vertical integration extends beyond these upstream functions to encompass the transportation of crude oil and natural gas, refining and processing into finished products, and the ultimate distribution and sale to the final customer.

Vertical integration was initiated by the Standard Oil Company under John D. Rockefeller during the late nineteenth century and has been a common practice of many oil companies for almost a century. For the firm, there is sound economic justification for vertical integration. Full integration from wellhead to gasoline pump provides a cushion against wide variations in earnings if one segment of the business undergoes a

19

period of relatively low earnings. At the same time, it provides for flexibility by furnishing the opportunity for exchanges of material with other firms, which allows firms to reduce transportation costs of shipping products long distances to meet marketing requirements. Because it is a liquid, petroleum lends itself to high-volume handling practices that apply equally well at different points along the chain from crude oil at the wellhead through shipping or pipelining to the refinery, and on to the marketplace.

Although vertical integration is attractive to the corporation, it does not necessarily have as strong an appeal to consumers or to the government. A more-fragmented industry structure may appear to be politically more manageable, and the possible extra costs may be worth bearing.

Concentration

Although most large oil and gas firms are vertically integrated, they do not control a significant fraction of the petroleum market.[1] In other words, there is not a high degree of concentration when measured relative to other U.S. industries or when compared to the usual definitions of concentration. The conventional yardstick used to measure industry control is that a concentrated, or oligopolistic, situation exists when four firms have at least a 50 percent share of the market in any segment of the industry. Measured in this way, the petroleum industry does not appear to be concentrated. But critics of this rather simple method of measurement such as James Flug and the late John Blair suggest that the degree of industry concentration is great because of the extensive use of joint ventures and partnership agreements by large oil firms.

Although no one oil company controls more than 9 percent of the American market in any one sector, the four largest petroleum companies control from 22 to 30 percent of the business in the four major segments of production, transportation, refining, and marketing. For American manufacturing as a whole, the eight largest companies hold a 60 percent market share, whereas for petroleum this ratio is 50 percent. Several major industries are much more concentrated, notably automobiles and aluminum, where the four leading U.S. producers in both cases hold a combined market share that tops 90 percent.

Within the United States, most of the drilling to locate and develop new reserves has been done by small, nonintegrated companies. These small firms often operate on budgets raised from private investors seeking the opportunity to risk income that would otherwise be subject to incremental, high rates of taxation. Fifty thousand wells are drilled annually in the United States, of which independents account for forty-two thousand (84 percent). Major oil companies, numbering twenty-one in an *Oil and Gas Journal* sample, drill the remaining 16 percent. Of these wells, about ten thousand are exploratory or wildcat wells, with 90 percent of these drilled by independents.

Retail-gasoline marketing remains one sector of the petroleum industry where the presence of the integrated major is highly evident. Integrated major marketers sell two-thirds of all gasoline through the pump, led by Shell and Amoco with 7.7 percent market shares. Partially integrated firms ("downstream" specialists) supply an additional 14.2 percent of the market, with the balance sold by independent marketers and cooperatives.

As an illustration of concentration in the industry, the largest oil company, Exxon, produces slightly more than 2 million barrels per day of crude oil and condensates, 3.3 percent of world petroleum output. Exxon, however, is not the largest U.S.-based producer of crude oil. Chevron (Standard Oil of California) ranks first among American producers, with 3.3 million barrels per day of net liquids production from all sources.

Studies of the twenty-seven leading American oil companies, measured in terms of total assets, show that these firms have a worldwide combined net liquids production of 16.2 million barrels per day (27 percent of world output). Their share of world refining is slightly greater, with the same twenty-seven firms indicating crude runs of 20.6 million barrels per day, accounting for a bit more than 30 percent of world refining throughput. Sales by these firms of refined products are 24 million barrels per day.

Because the United States depends upon crude-oil imports to supply about 40 percent of its daily requirements of 18 million barrels, it is relevant to consider the share of world oil reserves controlled by leading integrated U.S. oil companies. During recent years, these firms have become a diminishing factor in controlling world oil and gas reserves because of the rise of state-owned oil companies in the petroleum-exporting countries that have taken control of their national oil and gas reserves. The twenty-seven largest American-based petroleum companies have estimated oil reserves of some 44.4 billion barrels, 8 percent of proven petroleum reserves in the non-Communist countries. These same companies have estimated proven natural-gas reserves of 120 trillion cubic feet worldwide, or less than 5 percent of non-Communist proven gas reserves.

Coal Industry

Vertical Integration

The rationale for vertical integration does not apply today for most other energy sources. For example, coal does not lend itself to economic shipping over long distances because it is a solid and because of its low Btu content per pound. About 65 percent of all U.S. coal is shipped from the mine by rail. In addition, extensive coal reserves throughout the country provide transportation advantages to local suppliers. Thus coal companies have tended historically to be regional entities.

Although coal firms engage in the exploration and production of coal and its preparation for marketing, their involvement in marketing is not as extensive as is common with petroleum products. Historically coal companies had major commercial and home markets that were supplied principally by resellers. These markets were lost a generation ago as the popularity of oil and natural gas as space-heating fuels rose.

The major market for U.S. coal is in the generation of electricity by public utilities. Whereas in 1950 electric utilities used less than 20 percent of U.S. coal mined, power plants now account for three-quarters of all domestic coal consumed. Coal-mining companies have acted as fuel suppliers to the utilities but are not otherwise directly involved in this heavily regulated industry.

Captive Coal Mines

To a limited degree, utilities have been integrating backward by acquiring coal reserves and operating coal mines to meet their own steam-generating needs. The use of these captive mines as coal sources has grown noticeably since the Arab oil embargo of 1973–1974. Captive coal mines owned by utilities produced an annual average of 14 million tons during the five years 1966–1970, which amounted to 2.5 percent of total U.S. bituminous-coal production and 4.8 percent of the coal consumed by the utility sector. During the next five years, 1971–1975, utility-owned coal mines produced an annual average of 24.6 million tons, or 4.1 percent of U.S. soft-coal output and 6.7 percent of utility use. Currently utilities are mining over 50 million tons annually, meeting about 10 percent of their requirements from these internal sources.

Although it may be possible for a utility to cut its fuel bill by mining some or all of its own coal, the electric utility rate-making process permits utilities to incorporate their mining costs into their electricity charges. This arrangement can mean that an inefficient coal-mining utility may pass its costs on to the consumers, avoiding the necessity of closing marginal mines.

Other major coal users have also integrated backward into the ownership of captive mines. Railroads once were a major factor in coal mining, producing 22 percent of all U.S. coal (131 million tons per annum) during the years 1943 and 1944. The other major industry to employ captive coal sources is steel. American iron and steel makers have mined part of their coal requirements for many years, particularly the high-grade metallurgical coking coals used for the reduction of ore in the steel-making process. Steel companies are mining approximately 55 million tons of coal annually, a tonnage that has been declining slowly since the late 1960s in reflection of reduced steel making under the pressure of foreign steel imports. Between 1972 and 1976, steel companies supplied 60 percent of their coal requirements from captive sources.

The rise of captive mines owned by utilities has acted to offset the end of railway use of coal and the slow decrease in captive coal making by steel. Since the mid-1950s, the amount of bituminous coal mined from captive sources in the United States has varied from 13.2 to 18.0 percent of annual production.

Uranium Exploration and Production

The commercial situation in uranium exploration and production is quite different from the fossil-fuels industry in that integration is limited to activities prior to the enrichment of uranium oxide into uranium fluoride. The federal government maintains a monopoly on the enrichment of uranium, precluding any private-sector involvement at this time. Because the nuclear fuel rods made from enriched uranium are used in power plants for electricity generation, firms that manufacture nuclear reactors have also shown an interest in uranium supplies. However, the uranium-supply business remains separated from these nonmilitary markets.

Rise of Horizontal Integration

Although the growth of vertically integrated energy firms dates back a century, the emergence of horizontal integration as a factor in U.S. energy commerce is much more recent. In fact the acquisition by oil firms of coal reserves did not begin in earnest until the early 1960s. At that time, the coal industry was suffering a period of deep retrenchment, and the earnings outlook was not judged to be particularly good in the short term. However, some oil-company executives perceived the opportunity to acquire substantial energy reserves in place at a relatively low cost and made appropriate strategic investment decisions.

Involvement in uranium by oil companies dates to approximately the same time, although the incentives were significantly different. Extension into uranium exploration and production resulted from the economic gains that were expected to be made quickly from rapid growth of atomic power. Long-term prospects for nuclear-generation capacity were also believed to be excellent. Events of recent years have dimmed these expectations, but the incentive to apply existing technical skills in uranium exploration remains for U.S. oil companies. Oil firms also have entered into coal and uranium mining in an effort to diversify their fuel sources by investing against the day when their oil and gas production may decline as reserves are consumed.

Horizontal integration by oil firms has brought some political opposition to this trend mainly in Congress on grounds that this control of various energy reserves could result in price manipulation by the withholding of one energy source to drive up the price of alternative energy sources. Hence legislative proposals have been considered to achieve horizontal divestiture.

Coal

Examination of the horizontally integrated energy companies—particularly the consequence of the move into coal by firms that were historically oil oriented—shows that these oil companies today control 14 percent of U.S. coal reserves. Their share of coal production is about one-fifth of annual U.S. output. The twenty largest U.S. coal companies, regardless of parentage, mine about half of the bituminous coal, and coal mines controlled by oil companies account for about one-third of this fraction.

For the most part, the U.S. coal industry remains a relatively fragmented business controlled by regional firms that market to customers within a restricted distribution radius. Approximately five thousand coal mines, owned by several thousand companies, are operating in the United States. Although the average size of a U.S. coal mine is under 150,000 tons per annum, over half of the coal is produced from mines with outputs in excess of 500,000 tons per annum.

The coal-reserve base of the United States is held by many firms. The top twenty coal-mining companies, holding 21 percent of mineable reserves, include energy producers, railroads, steel companies, and utilities. The four largest holdings of coal within the private sector account for 10 percent of national proven reserves. These four firms include one energy producer (Consolidation Coal, a subsidiary of Conoco Inc.), two railroads (Burlington Northern and Union Pacific), and one independent coal company (Peabody Coal). The federal government remains the largest factor in coal ownership, accounting for 55 percent of estimated

U.S. proven reserves through its management of public lands in the western states.

Uranium

The exploration for and mining of uranium ore involves fewer companies but exhibits some of the same patterns of integration that are noticed in coal. Currently, approximately one hundred companies are exploring for uranium in the United States; approximately one-quarter of these are linked to oil firms. The production of uranium oxide, or yellowcake, is accomplished by some twenty different companies, of which five are oil companies. Taken together, these five companies account for about half of the uranium oxide that is mined and milled, because one firm, Kerr-McGee, produces about one-quarter of U.S. output. It can be argued that Kerr-McGee is more of a uranium producer than a petroleum company. It produces less than 0.5 percent of U.S. oil and gas, although that is enough to rank it twenty-second among U.S. oil firms, as measured in terms of total assets (which includes its mining activities).

The attraction of uranium exploration to oil companies may be attributed to the fact that 95 percent of all U.S. uranium reserves are located in sedimentary sandstone formations that are geologically similar to those containing oil and gas. Over the years, oil companies have discovered about half of all U.S. uranium reserves.

Other Fuels

Horizontal integration into more exotic energy sources such as solar and geothermal energy has been slow and selective. Solar energy does not lend itself particularly well to the application of the financial and technical skills possessed by oil companies. Unlike the large capital-intensive ventures of the petroleum industry, solar investments are on a much smaller scale at this time. Perhaps most important, the earth-science talents employed in oil and gas development are not transferable to solar, which relies more on mechanical and electrical engineers for its research efforts.

Geothermal-energy utilization, on the other hand, begins with geological exploration and the drilling of wells. To the extent that it can be practiced economically in the United States, it has been the province of oil companies. However, there are relatively few geographic regions where prospects suggest that a commercial geothermal project is feasible. This physical limitation of sites has restricted the enthusiasm of some firms to take a position in geothermal energy.

Profitability

The major oil companies have been subject to considerable adverse publicity because their net income after tax is quite sizable. But routine monthly surveys issued by Citibank indicated that ninety-four oil companies earned $15 billion in 1978, up 12 percent from 1977, while earnings for all U.S. manufacturing rose 17 percent. The percentage return on net worth for these oil companies was 14.3 percent, versus 15.9 percent for a group of almost fifteen hundred leading manufacturing corporations. Oil companies note that their profit levels reflect the magnitude of their operation and point to the return on stockholders' equity as an indication that their overall profit levels are in line with American industrial averages.

For 1978, the twenty-seven largest U.S. petroleum companies generated net profits of $13.6 billion on assets employed of $229 billion. Their return on total assets was under 6 percent, in line with their performance of one year earlier. Measured as a return on stockholders' equity, these twenty-seven firms generated a 12.9 percent return, slightly less than normal for U.S. manufacturing over the past decade.

The return on stockholders' equity varied according to the risk-taking propensity of the individual firms and the impact that governmental controls has had on their operations. For example, the highest return on stockholders' equity in 1978 was achieved by Louisiana Land and Exploration, a predominantly upstream company. Those companies weighted toward refining and marketing, where price and allocation controls have led to returns that have been substantially below par in recent years, yielded a return on stockholders' equity that was significantly below the national average.[2]

Examples of Horizontal Integration

In order to appreciate the rationale for the creation of energy conglomerates, it is best to examine selected examples of horizontal integration. The examples presented here indicate the variety of approaches that have been taken since 1965 or so in the expansion by these corporations to touch most forms of commercial energy production in the United States.

As measured in terms of production of the four main extractive fuels—oil, gas, coal, and uranium—the most evenly balanced of the horizontally integrated energy companies is Conoco Inc. Originating as a petroleum marketer in the Rocky Mountains during the 1870s, Conoco grew through a series of mergers and acquisitions to be a fully integrated domestic oil company, with a western regional emphasis, by the 1940s.

Following World War II, Conoco embarked on an aggressive over-seas-exploration program that resulted in large discoveries of crude oil in Libya. The erection of import barriers to block lower-cost foreign oil from entering the United States in uncontrolled volumes during the 1950s caused Conoco to buy a marketing position in Western Europe in order to sell this North African crude. Almost all of the European market toehold was obtained by the purchase of existing local companies in the United Kingdom, Germany, Belgium, Ireland, and Sweden. Refining capacity to service these markets was built during the 1960s in the United Kingdom and Germany. During the five years 1974–1978, worldwide petroleum production averaged 458,000 barrels per day, excluding purchases from host governments, and national gas deliveries averaged 1,571 million cubic feet daily.

The first major step toward horizontal integration was the acquisition of Consolidation Coal (Consol) in 1966 through a production-payment arrangement. At the time of the merger, U.S. coal earnings were yet to recover from a postwar loss of markets to less-expensive and more-convenient alternative-energy sources, such as petroleum and natural gas. Conoco executives reasoned that the long-term outlook for coal warranted the timely purchase of established mines that offered immediate income, coal-mining managerial expertise, and substantial proven reserves of energy for the future. Consol has retained a leading position within the U.S. coal industry since being purchased by Conoco. Estimated coal reserves are 14.9 billion tons, ranking Consol first in terms of privately controlled coal reserves. Annual coal production, centered mainly on Appalachian underground mines, has been around 50 million tons, giving Consol a 6 percent share of the national market and second ranking behind the independent Peabody in terms of annual tonnage mined.

Conoco also is a factor in U.S. uranium. It entered in the late 1960s and in 1972 opened a joint-venture mine and mill in southern Texas. Uranium concentrate sales in the five years 1974–1978 have averaged 500 tons annually and provided some 4 percent of national annual demand for uranium oxide in the period. Other uranium-ore deposits are being considered for commercial development in New Mexico and other western states, and it is probable that Conoco will remain a factor in domestic uranium supply. Conoco also has the potential of entering overseas uranium mining. A large ore body in Niger is being appraised for a possible joint venture by Conoco, the French atomic-energy agency, and the government of Niger.

During the three years 1976–1978, gross revenues from coal averaged $1.2 billion and accounted for 13 percent of Conoco corporate revenues. Minerals activities, essentially all uranium, have remained quite modest, generating under $11 million in annual revenues during this period.

Other examples of coal acquisition through direct means include the purchase by Gulf Oil of Pittsburg & Midway, the purchase of Island Creek by Occidental, and the purchase of Old Ben Coal by Standard Oil of Ohio, itself now 52 percent owned by British Petroleum. Old Ben Coal and Sohio provide an interesting case study on the relative scale of large firms in the oil and coal industries. Sohio, with annual revenues of $5.2 billion in 1978 versus $2.9 million two years earlier, is enjoying a sales and earnings surge resulting from its 53.2 percent stake in the Alaskan North Slope oil fields. Sohio proven reserves in Alaska are 4.1 billion barrels of crude and 6.4 trillion cubic feet of natural gas. Crude-oil production in 1978 was 507,000 barrels per day from Alaska, over 95 percent of Sohio's petroleum production in the United States.

With assets of $8.3 billion, Sohio ranked among the twenty largest U.S. firms at the end of 1978, and its net income after tax of $450 million placed the firm twenty-fifth overall among all American corporations. Yet measured against its peer group of other energy companies, Sohio appears as merely another middle-sized operation, despite its Alaskan position. Ranked against U.S. energy concerns only, Sohio in 1978 rated tenth place in terms of assets employed and twelfth place in terms of net income after tax.

Both Old Ben, and its parent Sohio, hold relatively important positions within their respective energy fields, but the absolute scale of the activities conducted by Old Ben is much smaller. Old Ben ranked twelfth among U.S. coal producers in 1977, producing 1.4 percent of U.S. bituminous coal output. With proven coal reserves of slightly more than 900 million tons, and 1978 mine output of 7.8 million tons, Old Ben has one of the lowest ratios of reserves to production in U.S. coal. The nominal reserves-production ratio for Old Ben is over one hundred years but is in fact much lower when allowance is made for future growth in production and the possession of coal blocks in tracts that do not lend themselves to economic mining units.

Gross revenues from Old Ben sales during the three years 1976–1978 averaged $160 million, or 4 percent of Sohio corporate revenues. With the trans-Alaskan pipeline now fully operational and Sohio throughput averaging 560,000 barrels per day, Old Ben will account for only 3 percent of corporate revenues in the near future.

Not all oil companies have gone into coal by the direct acquisition of operating mines. In cases involving very large oil firms such as Mobil, the outright purchase of a coal company might have been challenged as anticompetitive by the Federal Trade Commission or Department of Justice. Instead Mobil has been acquiring coal reserves on private and public lands in the western states on their own account. Mobil has reserves estimated at 3.6 million tons but has emphasized the purchase of domestic oil and gas acreage over coal in its strategic energy planning. For example, in 1978 Mobil outbid Gulf, Tenneco, and Southland to take over General Crude Oil, a subsidiary of International Paper, for $800 million. For this sum, Mobil will add 79 million barrels of crude oil, or 10 percent, to its domestic reserves plus 350 billion cubic feet of natural gas, or roughly 5 percent of its U.S. gas reserves.

Atlantic Richfield and Standard Oil of California used another approach to horizontal integration. Arco, which has been buying coal reserves in the western states, bought 27 percent of Anaconda in 1975 and completed the purchase for $600 million in 1977 to become a major producer of uranium oxide, as well as several key nonferrous metals, including copper and aluminum.

Chevron, through its acquisition in 1974 of 21 percent of the common stock of Amax, Inc., has a sizable holding in the third largest coal producer in the United States. Amax coal production is expected to be more than 40 million tons in years not affected by miners' strikes. Chevron made a $1.75 billion bid in 1978 for the balance of outstanding Amax shares, which was not accepted, but the chance of another takeover attempt cannot be ruled out.

The three largest California-based energy firms, Arco, Chevron, and Union Oil, have been among the most active in the fields of solar and geothermal energy. Their interest is only partly attributable to the location of their head offices, although the western states do contain most of the nation's geothermal reservoirs. Socal (Chevron), with over 300,000 acres of geothermal leases, is investing in a project to supply geothermal steam to a small electric power plant being built by Southern California Edison and scheduled to service about fifty thousand people when it goes into operation in late 1982. Generally solar and geothermal investments remain relatively small-scale endeavors for all major energy corporations.

Joint Ventures

Integration and diversification has been achieved by joint ventures as well as by wholly owned activities. Generally the use of the joint-venture technique in the United States has been confined by most integrated energy corporations to spreading the economic burden in low-risk, controlled rate-of-return ventures involving large capital outlays, such as pipelines. The trans-Alaska pipeline is an excellent recent example. Also joint ventures have been used to spread the economic risk in high-cost offshore exploration drilling, for example, in the Baltimore Canyon offshore New Jersey.

Joint ventures in exploration and production have been a common feature of oil-industry investment behavior abroad for decades. Joint ventures overseas offer the additional benefit of reducing some of the political risk in dealing with host governments that may impose unilateral changes in concessions or contract terms.

There have been historical refining-marketing joint ventures of note during the postwar decades. In the Eastern Hemisphere, Caltex was a partnership of Chevron and Texaco. The two firms divided up Caltex holdings in the early 1960s. Selective downstream joint ventures still exist abroad in consortial refining facilities, distribution, and terminaling.

Trends in Integration

The fifteen largest energy-producing companies in the United States produce two-fifths of all U.S. energy, measured in terms of Btus. The largest energy producer, Exxon, produces 3.7 quadrillion Btu, or 6.0 percent of domestic energy output, reports the American Petroleum Institute. In 1977, a typical record year, API indicated that the top eight U.S. energy producers accounted for 17.4 quadrillion Btu, or 28 percent of American energy production. This share was slightly less than that sustained a few years earlier. For example, the leading eight energy firms produced 29.6 percent of U.S. energy in 1970; in 1960 the share was 21.8 percent. Interestingly only five of the eight 1960 leaders were among the 1970 leaders. Seven of the 1970 group remained in 1977.

The future trend of integration by the larger energy firms is not entirely clear. Insofar as the non-oil companies are concerned, those that are primarily involved in coal, uranium, or alternative energy sources to fossil fuels show little evidence that they will be capable of making an appreciable mark in the oil and gas industry.

There may be some further backward integration by electric utilities into captive coal mining, continuing the expansion that was stimulated by the 1973–1974 Arab oil embargo. Today API estimates some thirty-seven utilities control 5 percent of U.S. coal reserves, and continued additions to captive coal production are expected.

Not all large oil companies have aspirations to be horizontally integrated in the near future. Texaco is a case in point. With assets in 1978 exceeding $20 billion and net income after taxes declining to nearly $850 million, Texaco's annual report showed the return on assets employed slumped to 4.2 percent, the lowest of the fifteen largest U.S. oil firms. This turn of events is noteworthy because Texaco had been an industry leader in return on assets. Texaco has stated that its main activity will continue to be the production, refining, and marketing of petroleum and related operations such as petrochemicals. Research and investment is continuing into future development of coal, uranium, tar sands and oil shales. Texaco holds about 0.5 percent of total domestic coal reserves but is not a coal producer.

Some of the integrated oil companies have decided to specialize in one sector. For the most part, this has meant a systematic reduction of marketing or refining activity because the profitability of these operations has been subeconomic for most of the past decade as a consequence of federal price controls and allocations on finished products. But a contrary decision was taken in 1979 by Ashland Oil, which divested itself of its exploration and production operations in order to concentrate all efforts downstream. Ashland, one of the twenty largest oil firms in the United States, has long been a strong regional marketer in the Southeast, and its upstream properties were a relatively small portion of its $2.9 billion assets, compared to other firms of its size. A similar decision to divest oil and gas properties was taken in 1979 by Clark Oil & Refining. Citing an unsatisfactory return on its producing properties offshore Texas and Louisiana, Clark said proceeds from the sale would be used primarily to expand refining, marketing, and chemical manufacturing.

The probable tendency in the immediate future will be for the larger oil firms to enter coal, and possibly uranium, by internal growth rather than by mergers. Prospects for the acquisition of large firms are limited and may be further constrained by government intervention, which led to the divestiture of Peabody Coal by Kennecott in 1977 after a protracted legal contest, and the sale by Arco of selected Anaconda copper properties in 1979 after an inquiry by the Federal Trade Commission. Some purchases of solar-energy businesses can be expected, but these advanced-technology purchases tend to involve modest capital sums.

Large private-sector energy companies may choose to emulate Exxon, which has declined to follow the takeover route in energy because of the political repercussions that such acquisitions would generate. Instead Exxon has established its own energy subsidiaries. In non-energy fields, Exxon may prefer to acquire existing expertise by the takeover process.

As a whole, the nonpetroleum energy investments of America's largest oil and gas businesses have not reported particularly high profits. New entrants into coal, such as Exxon and Arco, are just now ending a series of unprofitable start-up years with the opening of western surface mines. Those firms with predominantly eastern underground coal operations, such as Island Creek (Occidental) and Consolidation Coal (Conoco), have experienced widely fluctuating earnings due to labor problems in the mines and on the coal-hauling railroads. Uranium mining remained marginally attractive for companies if their long-term, fixed-price contracts for uranium oxide did not permit readjustments and remained well below spot-market prices in the late 1970s.

Decisions such as the purchase in 1978 by Tenneco of the forest products firm Olinkraft for $460 million, and the abortive attempt in the same year by Occidental to buy the wood and paper concern, Mead Corporation, for $900 million, show a continuing latent interest in diversification away from energy.

The recent renewed interest in domestic oil and gas exploration and production, a function of rising prices and the anticipated end of price controls on crude oil and natural gas, may reverse the diversification pattern by attracting capital that could have been earmarked for further spending in nonpetroleum energy fields or in nonenergy investments.

Notes

1. See N.H. Jacoby, *Multinational Oil* (New York: Macmillan Publishing Co. 1974). Since 1974 direct marketing by OPEC governments and national oil companies has further reduced the market control of the large private firms.

2. It is not possible to examine the financial performance of a similar sample of firms in the coal or uranium industry because there are few publicly held companies that are not operating as subsidiaries of other firms—either energy conglomerates, utilities, or steel companies.

4 Relations with Government

The events of October 1973 were the catalyst for the most serious energy-supply problem faced by the industrialized nations since World War II. The Arab-Israeli conflict that began on October 6 escalated to an announcement on October 17 by ten Arab oil-exporting states of a progressive cutback in crude petroleum output, with embargoes to be imposed immediately against so-called unfriendly states, including the United States. Since the end of the embargo in March 1974, a number of significant changes have been attempted or have been proposed in the national energy policies and programs of the nations belonging to the Organization for Economic Cooperation and Development (OECD). These changes include broad measures, such as OECD's creation (with France abstaining) of the International Energy Agency in November 1974 as an instrument for cooperative energy programming, and the recommendations of President Carter to the U.S. Congress in 1977 and again in 1979 of a sweeping national energy plan for the United States. The intent of all these efforts is to protect against a repetition of the economic and social hardships that would be precipitated by supply disruptions imposed by the Organization of Petroleum Exporting Countries (OPEC).

Steps to reduce materially this collective vulnerability, as taken by the United States and the European Economic Community in particular, by necessity have involved the multinational energy companies domiciled in these countries. These firms include not only the largest international oil firms (Exxon, Texaco, Gulf, Mobil, Standard Oil of California, British Petroleum, Shell, and CFP) but also the state-owned or state-assisted firms (ENI, BNOC, ELF-ERAP, Fina) and a number of smaller American petroleum and natural-gas firms with significant stakes in other fuels, notably coal and uranium. The most diversified of these are Conoco (coal and uranium), Occidental (coal), Sohio (coal), and Kerr-McGee (uranium).

In spite of the fundamental similarity of the dilemma faced by the major oil-importing nations—how best to cope with the possibility of disrupted oil imports in the face of political uncertainties—it is noteworthy that the governments of the industrialized West use widely varying ways to deal with the multinational corporations when tackling their national energy problems.[1]

Fundamental Differences in Relations

A cursory examination of the methods used to implement energy policies in the United States and in the major industrialized nations of Western Europe indicates considerable variation in the ways these governments involve multinational energy companies in the formulation and implementation of national energy decisions. These variations are interesting because the same companies generally have business on both sides of the Atlantic. Although their relative market share and importance varies from country to country, it is mostly true that the large American-based international firms, such as Exxon and Texaco, are ubiquitous, as are several European-based groups, including British Petroleum, Shell, and Fina. In the United States, however, there has been an ongoing adversary relationship that influences the thinking and action of officials of the federal government and the energy companies. Public stances on national energy questions taken by American government leaders in the executive branch, such as the Department of Energy, and in the Congress are frequently highly provocative and partisan. Not atypical was a reference by President Carter in 1977 to "potential war profiteering" by oil companies.[2] For their part, the energy companies also present polarized viewpoints, particularly during early stages of public energy discussions. Rarely are both sides prepared to be seen as conciliatory in their early tactical negotiations over energy policy.

The strained relations between the U.S. federal government and the established energy firms is evident in the fact that numerous members of both houses of Congress have proposed or supported legislation that would force a number of the largest energy firms, including some that are domiciled in Europe, to divest themselves of selected commercial holdings. American antitrust sentiments are strong. The tradition of trust-busting, dating back to before the Standard Oil breakup of 1911, finds its present-day counterpart in measures that would require vertical divestiture of upstream and downstream segments of petroleum operations.

Another relatively more recent antitrust phenomenon is American horizontal divestiture legislation. The U.S. Senate has been asked to vote on this issue several times since 1975. Under these proposals, oil firms beyond a certain size would be prohibited from holding an interest in more than one branch of energy production. The legislation is aimed specifically at those companies with oil and gas holdings that have diversified into mining coal and uranium during the past twenty years. In a September 1977 vote in the Senate, an amendment to S.977 proposed by Senator Edward Kennedy of Massachusetts to require such horizontal divestiture was defeated.

In July 1979, Assistant Attorney General John Shenefield announced that the Carter administration favored regulations designed to prevent major oil companies from acquiring other existing large firms unless they can demonstrate that such purposes would be demonstrably beneficial to the national economy. This proposal to bar acquisitions by the eighteen largest domestic oil companies of other firms with sales or assets greater than $100 million is similar to legislation introduced in 1979 as S. 1246 by Senator Kennedy and Senator Howard Metzenbaum of Ohio. The Kennedy-Metzenbaum measure covers sixteen companies and does not include the provision dealing with enhancement of competition. A similar bill in the House of Representatives, H.R. 4748, the Energy Anti-Monopoly Act of 1979, was presented by Congressman Udall of Arizona. Both bills failed to gain any momentum in the 1979–1980 Congressional sessions and have expired.

The position taken by the Carter administration regarding conglomerate-merger legislation marked the first time that President Carter had supported any bill that would broaden the restrictions on mergers now detailed in the Clayton Antitrust Act. Shenefield, in announcing the administration position, said that the legislation would prevent large oil companies from purchasing other existing large companies unless they can demonstrate substantial benefits to the national economy.[3]

A different climate exists abroad. The relations in Western Europe between energy-consuming governments and energy-supplying companies is less strained. With certain exceptions, the Western European governments and both private and public energy companies show more flexibility in seeking to resolve differences. With the exception of France, the country of origin of these energy-supply firms has not been a major issue. American-based companies have enjoyed a comparable status to their European counterparts when conducting business in the European Community.

By way of illustration, in contrast to the enthusiasm of many members of the U.S. Congress for divestiture legislation, extensive vertical integration—and to a lesser extent horizontal integration—has been viewed by European Community governments as a commercial asset. Rather than attempting to penalize the larger energy companies for their diversity of holdings, European governments have been content to monitor this growth and in certain instances have become partners in such diversification moves. The move into offshore oil and gas exploration joint ventures in the North Sea by the National Coal Board, starting in the 1960s, is one example.

Because the same companies are involved in the energy industries of the United States and other OECD countries, it is interesting to seek the reasons for the divergence in national policies. Although recent rapid changes in the international energy industry may mean that history is no guide to the future, an inquiry into the causes for these differing national approaches encourages a look ahead toward the possibility of convergence or continued divergence of these attitudes. Also it is informative to see how the companies have responded to these differing governmental climates. Perhaps opportunities for harmonization of policies toward the multinational energy companies may exist that could result in benefit to both parties, as well as to the consumers of the energy-importing countries.

Commercial Context of Differences

The history of the commercial relations between industrialized oil-consuming countries and the energy companies active within their borders must be understood before alternative policy paths can be appreciated. Numerous historical accounts of the growth of international oil companies exist. There are also summaries of the political and economic interactions between the multinational energy corporations and host governments of oil-exporting countries.[4]

Although in past years, American international energy companies have received diplomatic and political support from Washington, D.C., in their activities abroad, there also have been restraints on international business activities imposed by antitrust laws and trading-with-the-enemy legislation, among other measures. In contrast, other Western energy giants, BP and Shell, receive broad support from their home governments. French and Italian publicly owned oil companies and the more recently formed British National Oil Company (BNOC) have been subject to governmental control but enjoy considerable autonomy in their commercial decision making, with the added benefit of state backing and financial resources.

Company-government relations in Europe have been changing in recent years with the advent of major new crude-oil production from the British and Norwegian sectors of the North Sea. The resultant availability of local crude oil for northwest European refineries has helped keep the overall reliance upon OPEC oil by the European Community at approximately 75 percent of their petroleum requirements. Both the United Kingdom and Norway have crude oil in excess of domestic demand and are using their oil reserves to generate foreign exchange earnings through arms-length export sales at world price levels.

Refining and marketing profitability in both the United States and Western Europe has fluctuated widely in the last few years. The price of gasoline in the United States has been controlled since August 1971 when

President Nixon froze prices on most goods and services for what was intended to be a ninety-day period. Subsequent regulations by the Cost of Living Council extended controls on refined petroleum through 1973. Then, in response to the 1973–1974 Arab oil embargo, Congress passed the Emergency Petroleum Allocation Act of 1973, which authorized the president to control all refined-product prices through September 1981 and established an allocation system for refined products.

When the allocation and price-control system was first established in 1973, it served a useful purpose. At that time, the United States was in the midst of a genuine oil embargo and a shortage of petroleum products potentially existed, creating a need to protect customers from unreasonable price increases while independent marketers and refiners needed assurances against supply cutoffs. With the end of the embargo in 1974, the need for most of those controls ended too. Nearly all petroleum products were eventually deregulated, but pressures from consumer groups made gasoline an exception, despite decontrol recommendations by the Federal Energy Administration and the Department of Energy.

One of the victims of the continuing system of gasoline price controls and allocations has been the U.S. refining sector. It has not been economically viable for many refiners to add the necessary gasoline-making capacity to produce the unleaded gasoline that is in growing demand by the motoring public. Although the demand for automotive gasoline may peak in the early 1980s because of an increase in the mileage per gallon standards, the Department of Energy reports that passenger cars account for only 70 percent of total motor gasoline demand. The balance of the gasoline is used primarily to fuel trucks, vans, and stationary equipment, and demand in this area is expected to continue to rise for some years. Consequently gasoline demand for all purposes may increase well into the 1980s.

The problem of producing enough no-lead gasoline is vexing. Environmental Protection Agency (EPA) regulations strictly limit the level of exhaust emissions of new cars. To comply with the regulations, auto makers since 1975 have installed catalytic converters in passenger cars, making the use of unleaded gasoline necessary. As new cars have replaced older ones, the demand for unleaded gasoline has risen sharply, according to the Energy Information Administration of DOE, from about 5 percent of gasoline in 1974 to over 35 percent now. It will approach 80 percent by 1985.

To meet the growth in consumption of no-lead gasoline, more refining facilities will be required to compensate for the less-efficient refining processes. The manufacture of unleaded gasoline requires extra processing and downstream facilities, such as catalytic reformers, to build up the octane levels. Thus more refinery investment is needed. Moreover the upgrading process results in some of the gasoline being burned away. Hence the more unleaded gasoline manufactured, the lower the gasoline yield from a barrel of crude oil, which means that still more refining facilities are required to offset the yield reduction associated with unleaded gasoline production.

Yet another reason for requiring additional refining investment is that future crude-oil supplies will tend to be heavier and higher in sulfur content. That shift reflects the increasing use of oil from Alaska and from foreign sources. Given the existing configuration of U.S. refineries, gasoline yields will be reduced by using these heavier crudes unless investments in new processing units are made to offset the yield reduction, as well as to desulfurize the crude oil.

Consumer groups opposing deregulation suggest that decontrol would raise gasoline prices needlessly. Acknowledging that the supply of gasoline will be tight in the early eighties, they point out that higher prices today will do nothing to increase that supply because it takes at least two years to build refining facilities. Therefore, they ask, why add to inflation by decontrolling the price of gasoline if such a measure cannot add new supplies quickly? But this view oversimplifies the problem. It does not follow that gasoline supply under decontrol would remain unchanged because some projects to add new supplies by clearing-up bottlenecks could be completed within two years. More importantly, however, operational changes by refiners could increase the short-term supply of gasoline further, provided there was an economic incentive to do so. For example, facilities could be operated at higher than normal levels. Maintenance work could be delayed and operators who have petrochemical plants could divert some portion of their feedstocks to the gasoline pool, given sufficient economic justification.

In northwestern Europe and the Mediterranean, on the other hand, refinery surpluses have been a major problem. European refineries in the late 1970s have operated at less than two-thirds of their total capacity, a sharp reduction from the early 1970s when an efficient, modern European refinery could expect to operate at 90 percent of capacity. Current operating rates remain around 70 percent of rated capacity, according to data compiled by the OECD.

Service-station operations for both oil suppliers and retail site operators have often been unprofitable on both sides of the Atlantic. The key cause has been too many stations built to service the motoring public. In the United States, a series of dealer-protection measures have been advanced in the Congress designed to ensure security of tenancy and to support the profitability of retail-station operators.

Coal, on the other hand, has become more popular because of the prevailing higher prices for oil and natural gas, and there are brighter prospects ahead. A substantially rejuvenated coal industry is foreseen in the United States, where the Carter administration's newest energy plan and some private forecasts predict that output may rise from the present 700 million tons per annum to approximately 1.2 billion tons by 1985. Achieving this goal would require a compound growth rate of 7 percent per annum in the intervening years, a performance that is unparalleled in the history of the American coal industry. Also serious obstacles exist to a near doubling of U.S. bituminous-coal output, including delays in meeting newly imposed surface-mining regulations, compliance with the Clean Air Act and other environmental laws, and the uncertainties about the ability of the American railway network to carry the additional coal traffic that would be generated. Nevertheless strong demand and the movement away from petroleum-fired plants present an outlook that is more promising than it has been for many years.[5]

In the United Kingdom, where the National Coal Board operates the nationalized industry, there has been a reversal of declining coal production in recent years by the opening of new collieries. British coal production, now 110 million tons per annum, is expected by the National Coal Board to increase during the next twenty-five years to at least 170 million tons per annum by developing new coal seams in Yorkshire and Leicestershire. The National Coal Board has short-term plans to add 42 million tons of new capacity by 1985.

The German coal industry, largely in private hands, also has ended a long period of contraction. Bituminous coal's share of total primary energy use is 19 percent, reports the OECD, from an output of over 70 million tons, versus a 36 percent market share from a similar tonnage in 1967. Lignite accounts for a further 10 percent of German energy supplies and has shown a similar decline in relative importance.

In France and the Benelux countries, coal is not expected to recover its lost share of the energy market. That area has serious physical limitations, such as thin seams, which result in unattractive economics.

The remaining major mineral fuel, nuclear power, has become a mixed state and private activity. In the United States, reluctance to commit to the construction of a breeder reactor is but one facet of general American uneasiness about nuclear proliferation. Public fears about radioactivity range from health questions to waste disposal.

European environmentalists have questioned the pace of nuclear expansions too. The European Commission and OECD expect the Community will have at most 90,000 Mwe installed nuclear capacity in 1985, compared with a post-oil-crisis target of 160,000 Mwe, which was reduced to 125,000 Mwe in 1976. It must be assumed that public nuclear doubts will be resolved in time, and either atomic power will again proceed or the need to substitute other fuels will be accepted. Currently a number of European countries are dependent to a greater degree than the United States for electric supplies from atomic sources. In 1976 the Department of Energy indicates that the United States produced 8 percent of its electricity from nuclear power reactors, with 42,000 Mwe capacity. In contrast, Switzerland uses nuclear-generating capacity to produce 18 percent of its electricity (1,000 Mwe), the United Kingdom 10 percent (8,100 Mwe) and France 10 percent (3,300 Mwe), according to OECD reports.

Causes of Differences

There are evident differences in the manner that industrialized nations choose to involve the same multinational energy companies in the pursuit of state energy policies. In part this derives from policy variations that come from structural differences between the countries.

The United States has one of the few true multiple-fuel economies. Barring Australia, Canada, and the United Kingdom, no other industrialized states enjoy the range of indigenous fuel options open to the United States. In addition, a vast number of relatively small energy companies are engaged in all aspects of energy production, distribution, and marketing. These smaller firms are found in the petroleum industry, as well as in the exploration and mining of uranium ore.

Within the United States, the social desirability of permitting the largest energy companies to produce more than one fuel has been challenged increasingly in recent years. Aside from existing legislative and regulatory authority, there have been repeated attempts at new legislation in Congress that would require these firms to undergo horizontal divestiture of all but one energy resource.

The American populist resentment of big business is not as strong in Europe. Parallels for horizontal divestiture efforts do not exist in Europe because the coal industry tends to be either state run or in the hands of firms that specialize in coal. In many OECD countries, such as Japan, there is no large indigenous-fuels industry. Similarly opportunities for coal and uranium exploration and production are limited in Western Europe. As a result, the nation with the largest number of energy companies involved in more than one fuel is the United States, where one finds, in addition to the American-domiciled companies, the Royal Dutch Shell group and British Petroleum entering into American coal or atomic-fuels exploration or production.

As a result of the stalemate arising from the diffused system of government in the United States, with its large number of competing opinion leaders, the country has taken an inordinate amount of time in synthesizing a coherent energy policy. In part, this reflects the fact that the American legislative process arrives more slowly at policy decisions than does a European parliament; in part, it is because of the variety of options that are open to the American public.

There are also historical reasons for differing national energy attitudes toward the multinationals. Within most European countries, it has been customary since the early 1900s for the oil industry, in particular, to be dominated by relatively few firms, with a majority share of the market held by American companies.

Prior to the development of the North Sea, nearly all of the oil consumed by Western Europen in the postwar years was derived from imports. The governments of OECD oil-importing countries were alert to the balance-of-payment issues raised by the cost of these imports, even at the relatively lower prices before the Arab oil embargo. On the other hand, the United States is still adjusting to its reliance upon substantial quantities of imported energy at high costs. Some of the public have questioned whether oil imports ought to be the sole responsibility of the private sector.

Reluctance to continue past methods has been a motivating force behind occasional suggestions in the American Congress to create a federal oil and gas company and for proposals for much greater federal surveillance of contracts to import oil, on grounds that the oil companies may not heed American foreign-policy considerations. Oil-company executives hotly refute such suggestions.

Another major factor contributing to policy differences is the absence of a stable energy bureaucracy in the United States, in contrast to the older and more-workable civil services dealing with energy affairs in nearly every European country. Perhaps now that the U.S. Department of Energy has cabinet-level status, (since October 1, 1977), that problem eventually may be resolved. Nevertheless early prospects for streamlining American energy decisions at the federal level are not too encouraging because energy responsibilities remain scattered among congressional committees and within other executive branch departments. Such fragmentation is not normally found in Western Europe. More typical of the European models are the Ministry for Energy in the United Kingdom and the French Direction des carburants (DICA), with their professional bureaucracies and more centralized decision making processes.

Although the existence of an established civil service may be of greatest value during times of crisis, there is substantial benefit in the continuity of mundane day-to-day decisions and data collection that exists between energy firms and the civil service. Both sides thus have an opportunity to learn about the problems and competencies of the other. In this way, both sides have the opportunity to develop a working relationship before a situation arises that requires crisis management by either the public sector or the central government.

Influences for Change

Government policies toward private industry in Western industrialized countries are always evolving, and those with respect to energy companies are no exception. Recent events have caused all governments to reexamine the appropriate role for such firms within their national energy-supply pattern in order to ensure ample and continuous supplies of energy. Other influences also are causing changes in the working relationships between these governments and the multinational energy companies. As a result of these influences for medium-term change during the 1980s and 1990s, we can expect more radical breaks with past behavior in certain countries.

Within the United States a turbulent reexamination of energy policy is underway. The growth of environmental interests as a significant influence on policy, for example, has not abated. Nevertheless public awareness of energy issues remains rather low as evidenced by repeated opinion polls conducted by Lou Harris and other organizations that continue to show that barely half of the population knows that the United States is a net importer of oil. Efforts by Presidents Nixon and Ford to introduce comprehensive national energy policies all were thwarted. The current Carter administration has been only slightly more successful. Additionally both houses of Congress have offered alternative legislation, with the result that conflicting proposals frequently cancel each other out and cause inaction.

At the same time that this reexamination of energy policy has been underway, the American federal energy bureaucracy has grown substantially. In August 1977, President Carter created the Department of Energy with twenty thousand employees and a $10 billion annual budget, both of which have grown since then. Despite the lethargy of the Schlesinger years, it is too early to tell whether the department will be a focal point for American energy policy formulation or will provide merely one of several focuses for policy recommendations.

The American government's attitude toward the large energy companies remains ambivalent. Some proposed measures would severely penalize these firms, such as the vertical- and horizontal-divestiture proposals. Others would allow more-transparent accounting of financial results and special protective bills designed to support retail-service-station tenants, to cite a few recent examples. Phased-in price deregulation, however, certainly will boost company profits.

A third factor for significant change has been the creation of the International Energy Agency (IEA) within the OECD. The agency is supposed to provide the Western industrialized states with a coherent, group-wide energy policy, which affords them a united front in efforts at dealing with OPEC. Since its establishment in November 1974, the IEA has met several times and tested its capabilities under mock oil-embargo conditions. Despite the problems of the Iranian oil-exports curtailment when the Ayatollah Khomeini replaced the shah in 1979, the IEA is as yet to be tried under severe crisis conditions, and its ultimate effectiveness remains to be proven. It must be hoped, however, that the IEA will help to bridge any supply disruptions through the provision of a central clearing office and operations center.

Most of the success of any IEA efforts must be attributed to preexisting oil-company skills at supply and distribution, a fact recognized by the member countries of IEA who have worked closely with their oil suppliers in testing the IEA embargo mechanisms. Perhaps IEA is important also as a forum for governments and oil companies to understand their respective capabilities better.

A fourth influence for change in national energy policy has been the conservation effort, or more specifically the relative failure of conservation efforts in several key consuming countries. Particularly in the United States, a rather haphazard and lackadaisical approach has characterized energy conservation. In part the lack of success has been a by-product of the incoherent attempts at national energy-policy formulation.

Evolution of Policies

Prospects for the future suggest that the energy policies of the industrialized countries will converge in deciding how to use the capabilities of private energy companies. Several reasons for anticipating a greater agreement about the appropriate role of the private sector in meeting energy needs may be suggested.

In the United States, the energy civil service will mature, given enough time. As yet, a government career in America lacks the status appeal accorded in certain Western European countries. A pay differential versus private industry in America, insofar as the top jobs are concerned, also exists. Nevertheless over time the Department of Energy may attract and retain competent civil servants who can work constructively with private industry. Another problem in the civil service is the rapid turnover in staff, which results partly from the highly politicized nature of appointments. An end to this turnover would be particularly helpful for continuity.

In time in the United States, some form of a federal oil company may be created. Such a company is unlikely to be comparable to the government owned and controlled "flag" companies of Western Europe, such as ENI, CFP, and BNOC, and it is not likely to have the scope of a British Petroleum. It could arise from the federal government's setting up some form of a domestic exploration company to participate in outer-continental-shelf drilling, and from there a company with limited upstream capabilities might emerge.

There are no expectations for a direct federal role in coal supply beyond research work funded by the Department of Energy. This research sponsorship may lead to federal involvement in the manufacture of synthetic fuels from coal at some future date.

The continuation of efforts by the IEA and similar bodies to coordinate energy policy during times of crisis has meant a regular interchange of information and thereby a common basis for planning. Exchanges of data and viewpoints will homogenize some of the energy attitudes of participating governments and may result in converging views on the best way to maximize the use of the private sector in fulfilling the energy requirements of a country.

A third reason to anticipate converging policies is that most industrialized countries have increasingly similar problems regarding their need for imports of oil and natural gas. The United States will be increasingly import dependent into the 1980s, although it could enjoy slightly more flexibility if environmental restraints are eased to permit the development of coal and atomic power. Nevertheless the general trend toward greater imports of energy in the United States continues. Japan and most Western European countries are even more import dependent for their energy requirements. Among the larger industrialized European states, only the United Kingdom has prospects for net energy self-sufficiency during the next twenty years.

A fourth cause for merging national policies stems from the changing nature of the energy companies themselves. Until recently there was a wide difference between the activities of the established international majors and the smaller international independents. However, with the loss of upstream equity in the OPEC countries, the largest oil firms are now chiefly supply and distribution specialists and marketers. Consequently the majors now have more in common with the medium-sized independents than was the case fifteen years ago. For example, many independents and the majors have developed North Sea oil- and gas-production capabilities and, as already is the case in the United States, are now becoming vertically integrated in the United Kingdom. Of 6.6 billion barrels of commercially produceable reserves in North Sea fields held by North American firms, 52 percent are held by fifteen firms that are not among the five U.S. international majors.

Fifth, prospects for policy convergence may be accelerated by a growing awareness in the energy-consuming nations of the considerable opportunities for technical advances through the use of scientific knowledge found with the energy-producing companies. One example to consider, also from the United Kingdom, concerns the production of high-Btu synthetic gas from coal. Gas of a quality high enough to be injected directly into the pipeline grid has been produced at Westfield, Scotland, in a project involving the National Coal Board, British Gas Council, and a consortium of fifteen American energy companies.

Perhaps the most important factor contributing to a convergence of ideas on the roles of private energy companies in the industrialized West has been the growing acceptance by all parties of the need for mutual long-term planning on energy matters. Whether the planning takes the form of scheduling federal coal lands for leasing in the United States or bidding for drilling on tracts offshore northern Norway, there has been a growing, albeit grudging, recognition by industry of the government planning function. The relatively high cost of investment in a single major energy project and the long time needed to achieve its implementation suggest that allowances for the time and costs of government energy planning are now a permanent factor that private-sector companies should incorporate in their own plans.

Notes

1. Rather than attempt to present a summary of the governmental and public approaches toward large firms in each of the larger industrialized countries, selected examples will be used as illustrations. There is extensive literature on multinational corporations as well as accounts of the handling of the 1973–1974 embargo problems by various oil-importing nations. For illustration see N.H. Jacoby, *Multinational Oil* (New York: Macmillan, 1974); J. Blair, *The Control of Oil* (New York: Vintage Books 1978).

2. *The New York Times,* October 14, 1977.

3. E. Cowan, "Carter Bids to Curb Oil Companies," *The New York Times,* July 20, 1979, pp. D1–2.

4. For example see M.A. Adelman, *The World Petroleum Market* (Baltimore: Johns Hopkins University Press, 1972); F. Rouhani, *A History of OPEC* (New York: Praeger, 1971).

5. It is interesting to note that the present annual U.S. coal tonnage is approximately equal to that mined during the 1920s.

5 Public Energy Goals

Identifying Goals

The national debate about appropriate energy policies has commanded the headlines. Throughout this debate it has been implied that it is possible to have energy supply or demand goals that will be agreed upon by most of the general public. But perhaps it is wrong to make the assumption that common energy goals exist. Simply identifying public energy goals can be difficult. Usually these objectives are set by opinion leaders or by officials in industry or government who are responsible for supervising national energy activities. Less frequently, the goals derive from the general public and are tested by the democratic process. One example of this occurrence was the nuclear referenda that were held in several states, including California. The decisions by ballot on the future role of nuclear power are among the best examples of the direction of public policy being indicated by the voters.

For the most part in the United States, policy directives are set by elected or appointed officials who are judged at the polling booth on the strength of these and other decisions they made during their term in office. In addition, interest groups provide their own views during the national energy-policy planning process. These groups range from private-industry lobbying efforts, to environmental activist groups, to consumer organizations. Any member of the general public could belong to one or more of these organizations, although an individual might not take part in framing the energy views put forward by their organizations.

Public energy-supply policies are not only hard to pin down because of the manner in which are generated, they are also changeable and vary across society. For example, energy-supply goals, like other policy goals, vary according to demographics. People see their needs differently at different stages of their lives. In addition to the variable of age, the needs of individuals change according to their jobs, their personal income, their levels of education, and their geographic region of the country. The substance of public energy policies relates to the purpose that energy plays in our lives. Demand for energy is indirect; its role is to achieve other ends. People do not want power or the capacity to do work for its own sake, but in order to do something, such as to be warm.

Because the demand for energy is derived from other requirements and is indirect, it commands little public attention during times of ready supply and stable prices. Under these circumstances, consumers are not particularly interested in energy as a raw material; their attention is taken up by other matters. In seeking to identify public energy goals, we are mostly concerned with people acting as consumers of energy. In this role, they have multiple goals in life. They are doing many things at once, and their interests and priorities are constantly changing. To illustrate, the working head of a household with young children living in a northern community will have different energy-related desires to satisfy personal requirements than he or she may have forty years later if living in retirement, perhaps in a warmer part of the country, and in a small apartment. Although certain energy-related priorities may alter over time, however, others remain relatively constant. For example, that same person may continue to drive a car regularly to participate in community affairs.

The overlapping of activities creates conflicts of interest and usually causes individuals to take a different view about energy supply over time. Personal concerns change and emphases shift. Consequently one person may identify with different interest groups at different times.

Elected political officials and other public leaders are expected to reflect these numerous interests and create a consensus viewpoint on behalf of their constituencies. However, these leaders, whether elected or self-appointed, represent larger groups less personally. The problem is compounded by the existence of many sources of opinion leadership in the United States, with a fragmentation of special interests. Ideas are offered about energy supply, for example, at the national level in Congress, by the executive branch, and by many special-interest groups. A plethora of opinions can be found at the state and local level, too, with suggestions emanating from business, labor, consumer groups, environmentalists, and many others.

Given the indirect nature of energy demand and the complexity of public opinion and its tendency to change according to the special needs of individuals, it is not surprising that the identification of public energy-supply goals is difficult.

Public Preferences for Energy Goals

Security of Supply

One energy-supply issue that seems to be a definite goal of the general public is to achieve greater security of supply. A guaranteed, reliable supply of energy from whatever source stems from the desire to avoid the political problems experienced in the past because of uncertain supplies of this basic material and reflects national security considerations.

The sorts of steps that have been recommended to achieve greater security of supply revolve around reducing energy imports. In theory, reduced imports of crude oil and refined-petroleum products, as well as limitations on the amount of imported liquefied natural gas, may prevent the extreme supply disruptions that created chaotic conditions in recent years, most notably during 1973–1974 when Arab states embargoed deliveries to the United States and during 1979 when the overthrow of the shah interrupted Iranian oil exports.

A second way to achieve more security of supply is to diversify those sources of imports away from the OPEC countries. Although diversification may not save money—oil-exporting nations of every size use pricing techniques that reflect OPEC decisions—nevertheless some states are considered to be more politically reliable than certain OPEC members. Included in this group of countries are Norway and the United Kingdom, which share output from the North Sea, and Mexico, which has the added advantage of a shorter shipping distance for sales to the United States.

Many people believe that additional security of supply can be achieved by an increased reliance upon domestic sources of energy. Because almost 90 percent of the American energy resource base is coal, numerous political leaders have urged an increased use of this source of power.

In order to generate more electricity from domestic power sources, there could also be an expansion in the use of nuclear power from domestic uranium reserves. The public debate about atomic-power safeguards has taken precedence over the security of supply issue at this time, but the situation could change.

Another avenue for creating a greater security of supply could be through the acceleration of the development of synthetic crude oil derived from shales and from tar sands. Liquids derived from these sources can be refined into conventional transportation fuels such as gasoline and diesel oil. Synthetic gas from coal and other hydrocarbon sources is yet another possibility. Synthetic fuels, derived from coal or from tar sands, oil shales, or other hydrocarbon sources, can be converted into gases and liquids that are similar in their physical and chemical properties to conventional hydrocarbon fuels. For example, the use of coal to create pipeline-quality high Btu gas capable of being intermingled with natural gas has been under study for years.

Coal is highly suitable for liquefaction to create synthetic liquids suitable for refining into conventional petroleum products. The liquefaction of coal has been practiced over the last thirty years in South Africa, as well as during World War II by Germany. The technology is established but the economic attractiveness is marginal, providing small returns on large capital investments. To the extent that solar power, hydroelectricity, or other renewable resources can be integrated into the U.S. energy-supply picture, they can contribute to improved energy security also.

In his 1979 security proposals, President Carter stressed the need to accelerate the development of synthetic fuels. The Synthetic Fuels Corporation with its 12 year budget of $88 billion is designed to address this need. He also urged testing the economic feasibility of solar and the use of waste materials, as well as agricultural products, to create methanol from biomass as a potential transportation fuel. President Carter has recommended a massive program of federal assistance to develop technologically advanced sources of domestically based energy. His recommendation for the establishment of a capacity to produce synthetic fuels could entail the expenditure of $88 billion by 1990 in order to generate 1 million barrels a day of oil energy equivalence. In addition, he promoted the strategic petroleum reserve, which is scheduled to store petroleum supplies equal to approximately 120 days of imports, as an added security measure against potential crude-oil supply disruptions.

Predictable Prices

A second major feature of public energy policy is the desire for predictable prices. Budget planning for individuals, businesses, and governments is much easier if people know in advance what their costs of energy are likely to be. Avoiding unexpected shocks and seeking stability is an inherent human trait. People tend to resist change. For example, as gasoline prices rose by over 40 percent during 1979, many people showed their anxiety about future price increases by hoarding cans of gasoline, a hazardous practice.

In real terms, the search for predictable prices is separate from the desire for declining prices. Obviously everyone would prefer to pay the lowest price possible consistent with secure supplies for any material. In the case of energy, the desire for reduced prices on the part of individuals seems to be much stronger than the wish to have predictable prices. Manufacturers, on the other hand, might opt for predictable prices over lower prices.

Anxiety about energy prices leads naturally to discussions of appropriate conservation policy. There are headlines about "running out" and "a gap" when discussing energy supplies, or for that matter the availability of many other items. Concepts of the absolute exhaustion of raw materials date back to Malthus in the eighteenth century. Although the Malthusian idea of absolute exhaustion had its adherents, it has been supplanted in more recent economic thinking on the availability of fuel resources by Ricardian concepts of resources being available at increasing prices.

Setting aside questions of resource availability, it should be recalled that the cost of energy remains a small portion of the GNP, perhaps 8 percent. Consequently the cost of energy is not a major item in most household budgets, despite publicity to the contrary. The fact that energy may or may not be a dominant item in their budget, relative to food or shelter, should not prevent people from being gravely concerned about its current or future impact on the price of goods and services. On the other hand, an overestimation by consumers of the relationship of energy cost to their disposable income can cause an overreaction. Of greater importance to wage earners is the impact that higher energy costs may have upon their jobs. Unemployment due to high energy costs, plant shutdowns, or other labor-market dislocations is of far greater consequence than higher costs for domestic heating or transportation.

Related to the public quest for predictable prices of energy is the concept that there should be fairness in pricing. The idea of surplus profits, a concept of political economy, has taken root in the past few years following the 1973–1974 supply disruption. Earnings of energy producers have been boosted sharply by the higher income derived from the sale of their lower-cost inventory, and repeated explanations on their parts have not yet convinced the public to accept the claim that these profits are temporary. Whether the earnings from the sale of low-cost inventory at higher prevailing prices result in an immediate ploughback of the higher cash flow into additional inventory is of little interest to the public, which sees reported earnings by energy producers rising abnormally when measured in percentage terms against previous time periods.

Environmental Protection

A third clear public goal that affects energy is the desire for environmental preservation. People do not want to relinquish the environmental gains made in recent years as a trade to ensure lower costs or more-secure energy supplies. Although some adjustments may be necessary, there is considerable reluctance to reopen any discussions on environmental protection standards.

The interest in retaining the environmental gains of the recent past has a clear effect upon energy supply. The national attitude toward an improved environment also provides a good illustration of how other issues challenge the precedence of energy when public priorities are set. Throughout the country, clean air and clean water are prized highly. Legislation has been passed to ensure that our streams, lakes, rivers, and sea coasts are kept clean and that the air that we breathe is not fouled. Energy supply is made more costly, and sometimes curtailed, by these rules, as are certain aspects of energy consumption, particularly the use of coal by power plants, with its resultant clean-up of emissions from power-plant stacks.

The preservation of wilderness land is another feature of environmental protection that has held public attention. The desire to retain pristine wilderness, or to keep areas that are relatively unchanged by the impact of humans, is best seen in recent federal legislation designed to set aside federally administered Alaskan lands and large tracts of the western states by restricting access to industry or tourism. Although few people have the opportunity to travel to these remote regions, the commonly held view seems to be that these lands ought to be held aside from any disturbing impact brought about by energy exploration and development. This attitude has resulted in various restraints, including a suspension of the leasing of federally owned coal lands in the western states, and the withdrawal from exploration of over 100 million acres of public lands in Alaska, which might contain significant reserves of oil, gas, coal, uranium, and other natural resources.

Concerns about the environment have brought particular pressure upon the nuclear industry. Well before the Three Mile Island incident in Pennsylvania during early 1979, there was growing anxiety about the safety of nuclear-based electric power in America. Fears were expressed by groups who demanded safeguards on waste disposal, tighter controls over the proliferation of atomic weapons, and reductions in the risk of accidental contamination of workers who deal with radioactive materials.

Although electricity generated from nuclear power accounts for approximately 13 percent of the electricity generated in the United States, it remains unacceptable to large segments of the population. Some of the fears and resistance arise from a misunderstanding about the way in which reactors behave in commercial atomic-power plants. For various reasons, mostly concerning the environment, health, and safety, the expansion of electricity generation from nuclear power plants has almost stopped.

Despite the problems of nuclear-generation plants, of all branches of the energy industry perhaps coal has been hit hardest by environmental legislation. The public view of coal remains negative, with residual memories of the environmental disturbances of years gone by. Major new legislation such as the Surface Mining Control and Reclamation Act of 1977 has not yet allayed public aversion to coal as an environmentally unsound fuel source. Two illustrations will suffice. In underground mining, there is the problem of mine-water runoff with high iron content that threatens fish and plant life in streams and rivers near the mines. In the case of surface mines, there is the prospect of serious land disturbance, particularly in those western states in which the problem is made worse by the slow regeneration of fragile native plant life in some areas because of thin topsoil and low annual rainfall.

The petroleum and natural-gas industry has received its share of public pressure on environmental grounds too. Spills of crude oil offshore, caused by collisions of oil tankers or illegal tanker discharges, have been regularly monitored by U.S. officials in recent years and seem to be leveling off at tolerable but undesirable levels. Another risk is oil-well blowouts, such as occurred offshore Mexico in June 1979. The resultant oil slicks covered the western Gulf of Mexico. Onshore, oil refineries frequently are cited by neighboring communities as being responsible for unpleasant odors and air pollution.

Finally public-safety problems are engendered by storing liquefied natural gas (LNG). Natural gas refrigerated to 260 degrees below zero Fahrenheit is in a highly concentrated state, condensed to one-six hundredth of its normal volume. A leak or accident at such a facility during unloading of a supply vessel or during storage could result in a serious explosion because large amounts of LNG contain enormous amounts of latent heat.

Maintenance of Life-Style

A fourth notable public energy-related goal might best be described as maintenance of life-style. Most people resist change. This inertia in private lives, which is often seen in public affairs as well, slows down any shift in basic patterns of living. Insofar as energy is concerned, this trait appears as a reluctance to adjust the ways in which energy is used.

Resistance to change may be rooted deeply in psychological fears of dislocation, loss of status, or reduction in living standards. A desire to keep the style and substance of our lives is quite understandable. The energy-consuming devices to which we are so accustomed, such as air conditioners and automobiles, are taken for granted. Any radical alteration in their easy availability or commonplace use would be viewed as an unwelcome change by most people.

American economic growth in recent decades has been based upon the availability of an abundant amount of inexpensive energy. Particularly during the past generation of postwar growth, with its development of suburban towns and shopping centers and the expansion of long-distance travel by airplane, we have become accustomed to being highly mobile. We have also adjusted to the benefits of labor mobility that cheap travel provides. We are able to change jobs more frequently, moving from town to town or from state to state. The rise in the population of the sunbelt states, notably California, Arizona, and Florida, is attributable to the availability of cheap energy that permitted the conversion of sunny but arid climates into attractive residential regions.

It is easy to understand why the economically advantaged do not wish to relinquish the abundant and cheap energy that sustains their living standards. But at the other end of the economic ladder, the poorer members of society suffer the most from rising energy costs. The elderly and others on fixed incomes find it difficult to adjust to a significant increase in the real costs of energy on the scale that have taken place recently as the costs of gasoline, heating oil, and electricity have risen considerably.

The desire to maintain the life-style to which people have become accustomed, or hopefully to improve it, results in public energy aims that place a premium upon minimizing disruptive shocks. Schemes for transfer payments, such as energy stamps, are put forward in order to ease the burdens on those who are least able to cope unaided. Various direct and indirect subsidies have been proposed, and intricate interlocking programs have arisen in the effort to avoid the full and early impact of energy costs.

Personal Control

A fifth public energy goal that appears relatively widespread is the desire to allow a high degree of personal control over individual affairs, including energy questions. The attractions of personal involvement in small-scale energy management, or in the day-to-day affairs of any technical aspects of our society, arose in response to the thought that bigness as such is not a valid reason to justify certain social institutions.

The phenomenon of a growing rejection of bigness by the general public is widespread. Government, business, and labor unions are criticized as becoming overgrown and outmoded structures that are too unwieldy to cope with the requirements of modern society. One potential casualty of this growing desire for more personal involvement in energy affairs is centralized, large-scale electricity generation. Equally fashionable are energy-supply sources that permit the use of renewable energy. The growth of the soft energy path options, as advocated by Amory Lovins, among others, is a manifestation of the movement in American social thinking toward a less-impersonal system of energy supply.

Underlying the social debate about personal control over energy supplies is the assumption that energy supply is a social right. If it is agreed that individuals have a right to energy, analogous to their right to shelter, then the justification for transfer payments is immediately provided. Not everyone can afford to buy their energy supplies without subsidies. Energy stamps have been advocated as one solution, to be patterned along the lines of food stamps. No final decisions have been made yet by the federal government about the concept of minimum energy supplies as a social right. And related to energy stamps is the concept of an electricity lifeline, wherein the poor, the elderly, and others on fixed incomes would receive a guaranteed quantity of electricity in order to keep their homes lit and heated. Other alternative schemes to provide guaranteed energy supplies also have been proposed.

A consequence of the growing popularity of personal control over energy supply has been to make the process of energy-policy formulation a more difficult and extended job for policy makers. Many more groups now want to voice their opinions. Divergent and conflicting opinions abound. Treading a path through this maze has become increasingly difficult and accounts for some of the inordinate delays on decisions about where to develop energy-supply facilities.

Renewable Resources: A Case Study

The public energy goals illustrate that the preferences for energy supply are complex and in many instances involve decisions that are far removed from the theater of purely economic decision making. Many people seek to satisfy their requirements for energy with the minimum amount of effort. But they do not take the time or the effort to maximize the solution and in failing to do so are inclined to cut corners and sometimes to choose public goals that conflict with one another. This tendency to avoid addressing the need for a workable plan to secure the lowest-cost energy in the least amount of time results in a haphazard and erratic selection of public-policy options. If the problem were less complex or required less effort for its resolution, quicker answers might be achieved.

The current fashion for renewable energy resources provides a useful case study in the field of public energy-policy formulation. The vogue for renewable energy resources illustrates a popular policy proposal, but one with certain serious technical and economic drawbacks, as well as positive features. Although there are certain useful applications for renewable energy today, including the use of passive solar heating in design and hot-water heating panels to take advantage of the sun's rays in most portions of the country, it seems clear to this analyst that many of the recommendations for public or private spending on renewable energy—windmills, tidal power, low-head hydro power—could provide better economic returns if allocated to traditional fuel resources—coal, natural gas in particular.

By far the most popular renewable resource under consideration today is solar energy. Windmills, using air currents caused by solar heating, are a related power source. Installation of solar energy facilities is being encouraged by federal tax subsidies and even by state grants. The field is open to breakthroughs in low-cost technology, and many people are investigating ways to draw upon centuries of applied solar experience around the world in order to design energy-cost savings for the United States. Unfortunately the field is unregulated. Unscrupulous vendors of solar energy devices are selling unreliable goods and services to the public. For the most part, spending on solar-related energy-collecting devices is practiced mostly by those upper-income families who are interested in it as much for its "energy chic" as for its economic savings.

Water power is the other renewable resource that is receiving considerable attention. Although most of the massive hydroelectric sites in the United States have been dammed by private and public utility companies, there are prospects for small-scale hydroelectric generation, as well as the use of the ocean in various ways.

Three major ocean-related energy techniques are receiving the most attention: tidal power, employing barrages across narrow inlets; ocean waves harnessed by offshore baffles that would collect the energy in the open sea from the impact of passing waves; and the tapping of ocean thermal gradients to take advantage of the temperature differential between the surface of the ocean and the cooler sea depths, in order to generate electricity. Ocean-based electricity-generating systems are in an early experimental phase. There have not yet been any substantial pilot tests of these techniques. In the longer term there may be some prospects for this system, but more than technical problems need to be overcome. For example, offshore facilities would need to be protected against vandalism or accidental damages from passing vessels.

Another popular energy resource that is much talked about, if not actually widely employed, is the use of agricultural by-products and garbage to generate electricity and also to create alcohol-based transportation fuels. The burning of biomass or garbage in power plants has proceeded in a number of towns, with encouraging results being reported. Further advances in this area can be anticipated, if only as a means to dispose of garbage.

The formation of alcohol (methanol) from agricultural waste products or from grain that might otherwise be sold as food has been receiving wide publicity. The farm lobby sees the promotion of the gasoline-methanol mixture gasohol as a way to sop up surplus wheat and corn. In terms of cost-effectiveness, the economics are not good, but many people find it appealing, as is evidenced by the spate of pumps retailing gasohol through filling stations.

Renewable resources provide popularly acceptable answers to all of the public energy goals outlined in this chapter. They provide secure supplies, it is believed, because they are based upon domestic sources of renewable energy that are located within the territorial boundaries of the United States. They provide predictable prices because their major cost is in the initial capital outlays necessary to construct the energy-gathering device, and they are not highly sensitive to changes in operating costs.

The general public believes that renewable resources have minimal environmental impact. But in the case of some potential solar applications, such as central electricity-generating schemes, this is untrue because vast areas of solar-collecting material would need to be installed, owing to the low intensity of solar radiation and the physics of solar collective processes. Hydroelectric plants, moreover, ultimately silt up in back of the dams. There is no guarantee that these renewable resources will not be eyesores or liable to generate a good deal of air or water pollution.

Renewable energy resources score heavily in their prospective ability to help citizens live independently by providing personal control over energy-supply systems. Perhaps many of these sources would be privately owned and highly decentralized, without the impersonal features of large electric utilities or oil and coal companies. However, it is also possible that the way in which people live may be materially altered by a significant influx of renewable energy, particularly if it changed the mode of private transportation. Vehicles with rechargeable batteries or that operate from solar-collecting devices would be very different from the internal-combustion engine, to cite but one example. But there is no guarantee that there would be an equivalent or greater amount of personal control over energy supply if renewable resources became more dominant. Perhaps inherent economies of scale would lead to a new generation of large-scale central energy supply companies, similar to those now existing.

6 Public Energy Policies

Public Policy Prior to the 1973 Embargo

Not long ago, most Americans were unaware of the role that energy played in the national economy and the importance of secure fuel supplies to their well-being. Attitudes about energy supply and its corollary, energy use, were infrequently expressed by anyone other than those in the energy industry. For the most part, decisions about supply alternatives were left to the privately owned oil and coal companies, with public powers of surveillance vested in public utility commissions or other state entities, such as the Texas Railroad Commission. The development of nuclear-powered electricity-generating plants added another fuel option in the 1950s, muting the occasional warnings about potential supply uncertainties. Thus only scant attention was paid to the matter of deciding upon appropriate public policies to assist in providing adequate amounts of energy resources to meet national energy requirements.

This state of affairs did not arise accidentally or through oversight. At both the federal and state government level, policy makers were willing to allow private enterprise, in a relatively open-market economy, to make energy decisions. There were exceptions, of course, such as periods of severe energy oversupply as in the years following the discovery of the east Texas oil fields in the 1930s, when oil sold for as little as ten cents per barrel. In this instance, it became necessary that government intervene and implement some system of production controls in order to prorate output and guarantee that the oil-producing companies were protected against prices falling too far.

The private-sector energy producers acted no differently from their colleagues in other sectors of American industry by lobbying for various sorts of preferential treatment, such as the depletion allowance and crude-oil import quotas during the Eisenhower administration. As one consequence, the tacit role of the federal government became one of reacting, positively or negatively, to the requests of the private companies. Initiatives on energy-supply questions were rarely launched by either federal or state government. With the exception of wartime or other emergency periods, when governmental actions to alter the circumstances surrounding the supply of oil, natural gas, and coal were undertaken, supply allocations and policy adjustments were issues left to private industry.

59

This situation prevailed for the better part of a quarter century, but it changed dramatically with the landmark 1954 Supreme Court decision to establish ceilings on the price of natural gas, the so-called Phillips decision (*Phillips Petroleum Co.* v. *Wisconsin*). Those within and without the energy industry realized that this legal decision could (and did) result in extraordinarily low natural-gas prices. (National energy policy makers and advisers are still debating whether these low prices were beneficial to the country, by providing cheap natural gas, or whether they have had an undesirable impact in the long term by encouraging consumption of these energy resources at unsustainable rapid rates of increase.)

As U.S. petroleum production approached its historical peak in the early 1970s, imports of crude oil and refined products continued to expand in both absolute and relative terms. When it became apparent that American oil production from domestic sources would fall and would continue to decline, the principal oil-supplying countries raised their asking prices for crude oil but initially did so in a tentative fashion and by small amounts. Prior to this change of circumstances, the federal government's role was simply as an observer as those international oil companies domiciled in the United States negotiated with foreign host governments over concession terms and trading arrangements to the best of their commercial, quasi-diplomatic abilities. These abilities proved to be considerable, as indicated by the control these firms wielded in the crucial areas of pricing and regulating production prior to the onset of the seventies.

Direct federal intervention was generally avoided other than during the rare occurrence of an emergency, such as when Prime Minister Mossadegh nationalized the Iranian oil industry in 1951. Direct intervention also occasionally occurred as a result of industry violation abroad of domestic legislation. Under American antitrust law, it was not permissible for the international petroleum companies to coordinate their overseas negotiations and bargaining. However, both government and industry considered it appropriate for the private companies to act with minimal federal involvement in their international business affairs. This attitude was not unique to the energy business; it was prevalent also in the conduct and attitudes of many U.S. multinational businesses.

Thus relatively few public or political institutional energy-related arrangements were in place when the Arab oil embargo began. It became necessary to develop them so that the oil companies in coordination with their federal government could manage effectively whatever petroleum supplies might be obtained under the circumstances of the embargo. By and large, the international oil majors coped adequately during the 1973–1974 winter by using their skills in allocating fuels among customers in various countries. The shortfall was distributed among consumer states to minimize the adverse effects suffered by any one country.[1] At the same time a hurried series of international negotiations with other industrial countries in 1974 resulted in the creation of the International Energy Agency. Much of the credit for its formation has been given to former Secretary of State Henry Kissinger.

During the embargo the U.S. oil companies were criticized by the general public in America for having made energy policy decisions during the embargo, and for years earlier, without the prior consent or knowledge of the U.S. government. Although with hindsight it could be said that their historically high degree of commercial independence was perhaps excessive, they were at that time carrying out their functions within a context that was understood and approved, at least tacitly, by more than one presidential administration.

Postembargo Policy

The postembargo political climate quickly brought forward several spokespersons from Congress and many private citizens who demanded that the federal government take a much more active role in oil affairs to ensure that there was no return to prior operating conditions wherein the oil majors might behave in such a manner that might jeopardize the national interest. Definitions of national interest varied according to the preferences of the user, ranging from minimizing consumer costs, to assuring access to supplies, to guaranteeing "adequate" industry returns.

The historical arrangements had been irrevocably changed. No longer were only a few people interested in the subject of energy-supply policy. Everyone had been affected in some way by the embargo. Under the revised, postembargo conditions, it was no longer opportune for energy companies to conduct commercial affairs without a visible degree of government involvement. Whether the old nonintervention system could ever be reestablished to provide the simplest or least expensive way of securing guaranteed crude-oil supplies became a dead issue in the face of public demands for much more direct political influence upon energy decisions.

The historic concession agreements with host governments in and out of OPEC had been swept aside. This process had been a cumulative one. The loss of legal rights within the oil-exporting countries had been taking place for some years, most obviously as sovereign states created their own national oil companies to take over more and more responsibility for the production and export of crude oil. One outcome was that the economic incentives for the oil companies to behave as they had in the past were disappearing. Profit margins on marginal sales of oil were no longer as attractive, and decisions about crude-oil volumes to be lifted were now made by the oil-producer governments without consulting the Western oil companies.

Under these circumstances a sudden self-conscious awareness of a perceived need for a more-prominent federal role in energy policy determination swept through the nation in the early postembargo period. The willingness to allow the private sector to conduct energy affairs more or less as it saw fit was soon superseded by an avalanche of proposed remedial federal actions designed to make energy decisions more sensitive to public concerns over adequate supply.

Beginning in 1974, both the executive and congressional branches repeatedly reviewed the national energy posture. The Nixon administration concluded that a strenuous effort ought to be made to become free of the requirement for foreign energy imports. This brief flirtation with so-called energy independence was never taken seriously by Congress, the media or most analysts, who believed that the capital costs were simply too great to allow a forced shift toward more coal consumption, or the commercial development of extremely expensive domestic sources of oil shale or other substitutes for imported crude oil. Despite the OPEC price hikes, synthetic fuels were still more expensive, and the social costs of greater coal use, such as environmental damage, were not acceptable to many segments of the American public. Despite its impractical commercial aspects, the concept of energy independence has much political appeal. Many people, among them Republican president elect Ronald Reagan, still refer to it with the ideological conviction that it might be worth the economic sacrifice involved if America could thereby secure the political flexibility that would result from an end to necessary imports of foreign petroleum.

With the election of President Carter in 1976, the Democrats acquired control of both Congress and the presidency for the first time since the energy crisis arose. Hopes increased that more coordination and action to solve these complex problems could now be achieved. But it soon became apparent, with the first of a series of national energy plans, that there was a serious inability of the executive branch and the Congress to work together. Factionalism and regional differences surfaced and were worsened by the long process of formulating energy approaches that would bridge the considerable differences in outlook between the energy-producing and energy-consuming sections of the country. These differences were aggravated by the unprecedented amount of time that was spent on energy issues during the first years of President Carter's administration. Much of the Ninety-fifth Congress, from 1977 to 1978, was taken up by efforts on the part of the executive branch to get Congress to pass into law some form of highly structured and permanent energy policy.

Because of the complexity and scale of energy-policy development, it is not surprising that the Carter administration failed to secure congressional approval of any such sweeping national energy program. The inherent difficulties of the task were made worse by personality conflicts between the first secretary of energy, James Schlesinger, and congressional leaders, (who were not fond of his intellectual demeanor and characteristic inflexibility.) Personal interviews with industrialists and federal employees at many levels indicate he was a very difficult person for many members of Congress to deal with, and the issue of his personality became an obstacle to the resolution of certain problems.

While the symbiotic role of the private energy-producing sector and the federal government was undergoing serious structural reexamination as a consequence of the shocks generated by the Arab oil embargo, two other social trends were having their own impact on American energy-supply decision making: mounting concern for improved environmental protection and the belated recognition that greater attention to energy conservation could secure valuable additional time for the eventual transition away from existing energy supply and use patterns.

Environmental Protection

Although preservation of the environment and energy conservation are often linked in the public mind because the former is aided by the latter, the issues warrant treatment as independent topics. Let us consider first the matter of environmental preservation. It has been argued by energy producers and their advocates that incentives for new energy production have become victims of the growth of American enthusiasm for the preservation and restoration of the quality of our air, land, and water. Special-interest groups supporting stringent environmental-protection actions may have misunderstood and underestimated the differences between the physical damage caused by historical methods of energy-resource production and the improved techniques that are now employed to mine coal, uranium, and other forms of energy. Their inability to differentiate between past practices, judged as acceptable at that time, and what is now feasible is one factor contributing to the delays in arriving at a more satisfactory way to supply American energy requirements.

Previously widespread mining and oil-production techniques have been, and continue to be, generally conducted with the best available technology, consistent with economic sense and current social and legislative mandates, as well as the prevailing economic philosophy, which permitted the externalizing of costs in the past. As technical abilities advance and as recognition of the environmental damage caused by certain past practices grows, society usually changes the rules. The new ground rules of recent years contain a heightened sensitivity to environmental responsibilities. Concerns for the protection and restoration of the original terrain of resource-exploited lands are just one example. These new controls often take the form of legislative directives or regulations such as the 1977 Surface Mining Control and Reclamation Act rather than taxes or fees to abate the environmental impact. Direct regulation ensures immediate compliance by American energy producers, although the economic impact of such controls may be more costly than the alternative of regulations to induce appropriate investments by the private sector in order to reduce the levies imposed for noncompliance.

In the future, the socially mandated rules linking industrial activity and environmental protection no doubt will change again. Someday we may also reflect back on the regulatory systems in place today and consider them to be as inappropriate at a future date as would be the continuation today of procedures used a generation or two ago. There is no way we can anticipate accurately how public attitudes about current energy production practices will change for the future. For that same reason, it is unreasonable to be overly critical of the way energy was supplied in the past by invoking contemporary standards.

The search for a more healthful environment has moderated the precedence of energy supply as a key public priority. In time, that ordering of priorities may be revised again. Present decisions about energy are merely one set of choices among many types of policy options that confront the government and the public in a continuous decision-making process. Protection of the environment is now considered to be sufficiently important to retard the development of domestic energy from fragile lands and coastal waters. Consequently energy producers recognize that they have no choice but to act in accordance with the various legislative directives. At the same time, however, these firms vigorously point out that there are excellent reasons for the national concern with the environment to be subject to continued scientific study in order to quantify the impact of industrial activities.

The dynamism of the energy-environment debate will make further change inevitable and desirable. Furthermore as we move into the 1980s, environmental issues may be mitigated by growing pressures to solve energy problems. At present, various laws enacted at the state and national level within the last ten years indicate that the general public does not share the industry viewpoint that energy-production methods can be environmentally benign and should be less restricted.

The passage in 1977 of wide-ranging legislation covering surface mining and the Energy Policy and Conservation Act of 1975 are two illustrations of major federal legislation that protects the environment and at the same time places certain constraints upon the expansion of energy output in the United States by limiting effluents which industries can release into the air. These constraints are not insurmountable but have certain costs associated that add to the overall outlay for energy supplies. The Clean Air Act Amendments of 1977 and the withdrawal of very large tracts of land in Alaska in 1978 provide further examples of how Congress and the president have responded to environmentalists by acting in ways that foster the cause of environmental protection but carry the consequence of trading off potential energy output.

These decisions are all reversible, except for the lost time that cannot be recouped, if Congress was to decide at some future date that it was preferable to permit aggressive energy exploration and development programs. For example, on Alaskan public lands, Congress one day may change its 1978 decision to hold aside 100 million acres of this land and allow a resumption of the exploration for extraction of minerals and fuels from these properties. For the time being, the field belongs to the environmentalists, who have convinced the nation that Alaska and the rest of the country have natural beauties and life-supporting mechanisms that are neither inexhaustible, nor renewable, nor replaceable.

Concerns over the environment have alerted society to a possible danger. Thus the energy-producing industries must take some measure of environmental care in their activities, and the costs will be borne by consumers as direct charges passed on by industry. However, this state of affairs does not preclude a change in the current weighting of energy-environmental concerns. The present situation serves only to define the arrangement of priorities as it now stands. Also, because the environment is a comparatively new issue for general concern, because the public does not trust industry to set aside lands for preservation, the people through their government have ensured a degree of preservation. Government thus has acted where the private sector has no real interest, despite any public-relations protests to the contrary. As long as the benefit-cost analysis continues to be reevaluated and neither concern (energy or the environment) dangerously subjugates the other, there is ample room and flexibility enough for both of these legitimate concerns to be combined effectively.

Energy Conservation

Energy conservation must not be confused with energy decisions directed at providing expanded energy supplies. The greatest merit of energy conservation is to provide added time for the nation to adjust its economy to an era of high-cost fuels in the long term and to allow for reduced energy costs in the short term. Although it is true that energy conservation can reduce energy imports temporarily, conservation alone does not create the means to supply new energy from domestic sources. Simply put, conservation is the collateral against which more energy-adjustment time is borrowed; conservation can only go so far.

Energy conservation can become more costly than producing energy by going beyond the point of diminishing returns. For example, retrofitting insulation into existing buildings saves on energy costs, but the capital outlays required may not be recouped during the remaining useful life of the building. A more cost-effective conservation technique that also can yield comparable energy savings is possible by incorporating more-energy-efficient designs into new construction. Conservation by retrofitting, to the fullest extent that is economically feasible, makes sense in selected cases because the replacement of the existing stock of homes, offices, and factories by new construction would take fifty to sixty years. Thus in certain instances, conservation can contribute to cost efficiency over a substantial period of time. However, conservation is a stopgap energy measure; it is not a source of energy. Furthermore it would be dangerous to view conservation as a substitute for actions to encourage new energy production. Genuine conservation efforts and the realistic recognition of the need to encourage new energy production are two separate facets of the problem. They need to be integrated successfully and constructively into a comprehensive energy-policy output. To the extent that conservation can promote the more efficient use of energy and does not entail large changes in life-styles, thereby allowing us to get the same output for less input or more product per unit of energy consumption, it should be encouraged.

Synthetic Fuels

Congressional actions to supplement domestic fossil-fuel supplies have looked beyond short-term matters to embrace the promotion of synthetic fuels (from coal and other hydrocarbon sources), as well as various formats for decontrol of domestic gas and oil prices as a long-term move to generate energy supplies at prices reflecting their replacement costs. Synthetic fuels offer some attractive alternatives but cannot provide much short-term help in expanding energy supplies; the lead time required to place the most advanced commercial-scale facilities of this type on-line may be ten years or more. It remains to be seen what benefits will derive from the congressional passage in June 1980 of the synthetic fuels promotion steps embodied in the Energy Security Act that created the

United States Synthetic Fuels Corporation, the body intended to be the principle conduit for funneling federal support to synthetic fuels. Federal planners hope that these alternative fuel sources could yield the equivalent of 2 million barrels per day by the early 1990s.

As energy demand grows, or even if it remains stable, a decrease in supply from existing sources will require timely actions regarding supplementary and alternative sources to avoid energy-supply disruptions. During the transition period to synthetic fuels, which has now begun, continued reliance upon direct burning of coal, oil, and gas and probably nuclear power seems essential.

Price Controls

The Carter administration and Congress have taken definite steps to encourage the output of energy from traditional sources by permitting the phased deregulation of domestic crude oil prices. Under provisions of the 1975 Energy Policy and Conservation Act, price controls on U.S.-produced crude oil are scheduled to end in 1981.

Decontrol has been a very sensitive political issue, as many people believe that very high profits would be earned by the U.S. oil companies if domestic crude was priced at the OPEC-related price prevailing in world markets. Therefore in an effort to calm public anxiety over high profit rates for oil companies and to dilute opposition to price deregulation, the Congress has passed and President Carter has signed windfall-profits tax legislation designed to tax unearned profits that are not vital to corporate operations. Some of this tax money is earmarked for federal sponsorship of alternative-energy production means, and some of the revenues will be used for social-transfer payments and other public purposes.

Many people believe that it is sound economic sense to charge the world market price because the short-term alternative cost for replacing the marginal supply of domestic oil is to pay world market prices for imports.[2] Deregulation will allow the economy to deal more effectively with the true costs of crude oil by forcing Americans to pay world prices and realize that cheap oil is a thing of the past. Furthermore it is appealing to have American consumers pay the world price to American producers for three other reasons. First, it prevents undervaluing of domestic resources of oil. Second, although it allows U.S. firms to accrue larger than usual profits, a windfall-profits tax can recoup some of the additional income for redirection within the national economy, thus giving American consumers (and voters) a psychologically important control mechanism over energy production decisions. Third, it forces American decision makers and consumers to emerge from their cocoon of an isolated, protected energy market and realize the fact of rising energy costs as it has been felt by people in other countries.

Nuclear Concerns

The coal-atomic-petroleum balance of national energy supply was rocked by the nuclear accident in Pennsylvania at Three Mile Island during 1979. It is still too soon to judge what this incident will mean to the nuclear component of our fuel supply mix in the long term. Measures to improve the surveillance of nuclear power plants, to increase public-health safeguards, and to reassess generally the role for nuclear power are understandable in the light of Three Mile Island. In these deliberations, it needs to be remembered that if adequate controls can be fashioned, nuclear power may offer the opportunity to generate base-load electricity at quite low costs relative to coal or any other fuel.

American public utilities have few energy-supply choices open to them. They can use atomic power or continue to rely upon coal. (Under the terms of the Power Plant and Industrial Fuel Use Act legislation enacted in 1978, heavy fuel oil and natural gas are to be phased out as boiler fuels by 1990.) Direct burning of coal brings with it different environmental problems than would be incurred with the continued use of nuclear power. No matter which fuel option is selected, there is no way to avoid some health and safety risks.

Whatever the future for new nuclear power plants, there are already some seventy-odd reactors operated by U.S. utilities, so to dismiss the use of nuclear fuel altogether is not wholly practicable. One advantage of using uranium fuels is that self-sufficiency from U.S. resources of uranium oxide to meet the requirements of these plants may be achievable as more firms undertake exploration on federal lands in western states.

The existing federal monopoly on uranium enrichment and the complex process of making fuel rods has placed forward integration into uranium relatively low on the list of commercial ventures for most energy-producing companies. Of more immediate interest to them is the extent of any federal help that may be provided to the utility industry, so that public utilities may complete the building of planned coal or nuclear power plants according to a predictable timetable. Unexpected delays arising from lawsuits or because of pressures from citizen-action groups need to be minimized in order to permit an orderly development of energy-supply mechanisms. The uncertainty of unforeseen delays creates the most costly problems because of their disruptive influence upon financing and construction planning.

It would serve to mitigate some of America's energy-supply problems of the future to be able to make reliably firm decisions soon on nuclear fuel development, installment, and use. The very complex technical nature of the topic and public perceptions of nuclear power create an understandable uneasiness in the public mind concerning atomic fuels. More information and a much greater degree of public knowledge and debate on the issue are required before an informed and clear energy policy can be framed.

Notes

1. See J. Blair, *The Control of Oil* (New York: Vintage Books, 1978); R. Stobaugh and D. Yergin, *Energy Future* (New York: Random House, 1979).

2. R. Stobaugh and D. Yergin, *Energy Future.*

7 Performance of Large Energy-Producing Companies

It is a common perception that the giant energy firms provide the majority of America's fuel supplies. In truth there is a wide variety of firms, large and small, involved in supplying energy to American industry and homes. These companies include independent wildcatters, who drill but one well per year, as well as the larger, more-familiar corporate names listed on the stock exchange or selling energy products along the roadside. The resources of these companies vary greatly; however, despite all of the complex subtleties of the energy business, it is possible to determine if American energy-producing firms are pursuing policies conducive to achieving public energy-supply goals. Any measurement of their performance involves subjective criteria, but a good deal of evaluation can be based upon data about their performance. Such evaluations can highlight those areas where private energy companies have been most and least successful in achieving those goals that the general public considers relevant.

Oil and Gas Exploration and Development

One of the easiest methods of evaluating performance is to measure the extent to which efforts are being directed by energy-supply companies toward achieving a greater degree of national energy self-sufficiency. It is widely appreciated that American dependence upon imported petroleum has grown greatly and may continue to do so for some time into the future. In light of this, it is fair to ask whether energy producers have applied themselves with sufficient vigor to identify and develop domestic oil and gas opportunities. Finally, we should inquire as to how successful their efforts have been, relative to the past. In particular, data on the mix of capital investments and exploration expenses in the United States and abroad can show whether the private sector has increased its relative emphasis upon American energy opportunities or whether it has continued the pre-1973 Arab oil embargo pattern of diversifying energy investments around the globe.

An examination of the financial performance of the largest petroleum companies, such as that made annually by the Chase Manhattan Bank, indicates that these companies in aggregate have increased their relative expenditures for oil and gas exploration development and production, but with proportionally more stress on these activities outside of the United States. In 1977 these expenditures for the Chase Manhattan group of companies in the United States exceeded $15 billion, up 280 percent from 1967. If an adjustment for inflation is made by applying the U.S. GNP price deflator to correct the 1967 figures, the increase over the decade is a substantial 111 percent.

Outside of the United States the Chase Group reported the increase in expenditures for exploration, development, and production during the ten years is 381 percent, showing that there has been a proportionally greater effort made to find and produce oil from non-U.S. sources. The main reason is that oil explorers expect to earn more for a comparable risk taken abroad. In most foreign sedimentary basins, only limited exploration efforts have been made; in contrast, the contiguous forty-eight states have been carefully combed for drilling prospects. Additionally the fiscal and regulatory climates in many countries are at least as favorable as the situation in the United States; notably the regulations on pricing oil and gas are less restrictive. Taken as a whole, the incentives for oil and gas exploration abroad are excellent, and exploration budgets have reflected that fact.

Upstream outlays have been stressed far more than capital investments in the refining and marketing sector. After adjusting for inflation, expenditures in the United States on oil production more than doubled between 1967 and 1977, while in the same time period the constant-dollar value of downstream expenditures for refining and marketing did not change. Again, as was the case in the split between aggregated U.S. and non-U.S. spending patterns, the reason for the emphasis of upstream over downstream was that refining and marketing offered chronically lower returns, as evidenced by the Chase studies. Perhaps American upstream spending was stressed because of the persistent weakness in refining profit margins during most of the 1970s, with major companies (those of the Chase survey) generally abstaining from significant refinery expansions or the construction of new grass-roots refining.

Some companies with ongoing commitments in newly maturing energy-supply areas, such as the British sector of the North Sea, have had special reasons not to shift their investment emphasis to the United States because they have been seeking to increase oil output from other non-OPEC sources. Those firms investing outside of OPEC states, in areas such as the North Sea, are helping to diversify American supplies away from dependence upon OPEC, even if the actual energy-supply costs to American consumers are no different.

The popularity of non-OPEC foreign resources reflects several structural changes that have taken place in recent years, most notably the rise of OPEC as a factor in the world oil market, with the simultaneous diminishing of the influence of private oil companies in OPEC nations. The consequence of this power shift has been to encourage the private companies to increase their search for oil and gas in non-OPEC nations. This search has required exploratory work in high-cost areas with hostile environments, such as the North Sea and the Arctic. The economic justifications for these high-cost and high-risk exploratory endeavors come from the higher world price that has been set by OPEC and the continuing pursuit of secure energy supplies.

At the same time, domestic investments downstream have been cut back because higher petroleum prices have acted to dampen the growth of demand and limited requirements for additional refining capacity, tankers, and marketing facilities. This shift in emphasis has been most evident in the United States. In other countries, changes in the demand for different oil products, such as the shift toward middle distillates at the expense of heavy fuel oil, have meant that selected investments in adjustments to refinery product mix options and distribution patterns have continued.

Any individual company efforts to explore more in the United States have been overshadowed by the larger international opportunities that have been identified in new oil-producing regions of non-OPEC, industrialized countries, such as the British and Norwegian sectors of the North Sea and the Canadian Arctic. These attempts to diversify the sources of American petroleum supplies away from OPEC could carry the United States a considerable distance toward the political goal of reducing the risk of any OPEC-inspired supply disruptions. However, the national policies of these newer oil-producing states do not necessarily mesh with American preferences. For example, Norway restricts oil output and has been very slow to license new exploration tracts. British relations with fellow members of the European Community limit Britain's interest in crude-oil sales outside the Common Market. Canadian oil policies are well documented and show all too clearly how strained the relations can be between Ottawa and the provincial governments; these strains affect export quantities and prices.

Coal and Uranium Development

A different pattern is seen in the capital and exploration expenditures made for the development of coal and uranium reserves. The American coal industry has undergone a significant expansion in recent years, and production has risen to record levels. Uranium exploration programs have also shown strength despite the uncertain future for nuclear reactors; the number of firms engaged in this activity has continued to grow each year.

American multinational companies have taken little interest in exploiting foreign coal reserves because American supplies are more than adequate for domestic purposes. There has been some selective investment abroad in uranium exploration and production, but uranium oxide imports are as yet a minor contribution to total U.S. requirements. Much of the international uranium exploration work by U.S. companies has been low key and receives little publicity.

Spending by U.S. companies on coal and uranium production capacity, if anything, exceeds present requirements. Coal, in particular, is demand restrained; that is, there are more proven reserves of coal than necessary to support market demand. Uranium, too, has clearly moved into this category of relative abundance now that nuclear-power-plant construction in the United States has been temporarily halted in the wake of the Three Mile Island accident. Furthermore additional substantial reserves of uranium continue to be found in Canada, Australia, and western Africa, as well as in the United States.

Environmental Considerations

The energy industry suffers from the reputation of being a notorious polluter. The general public thinks of the energy industry's environmental record in terms of oil spills, acid mine runoffs, and unreclaimed coal land. Blowouts from offshore oil wells and discharges of contaminated ballast water by tankers are particularly newsworthy items. Are these public perceptions correct or unwarranted? Consider oil spills from tankers. Each year more than two billion tons of crude-oil and petroleum products are shipped on the world waterways. Of this amount, something less than two million tons goes into the sea from marine transportation. Although this represents but one part in a thousand, it is still enough to create a terrible physical mess and an environmental and economic threat to the affected coastlines.

Repeatedly the world has lamented the after-effects of collisions between tankers off the coasts of virtually every continent. The world's biggest single-vessel oil spill occurred in March 1978 when the *Amoco Cadiz* ran aground off the French coast. As a result of that accident, 230,000 tons of Saudi Arab light crude oil spilled out onto sixty miles of French beaches and precipitated claims amounting to more than $83 billion. These claims far exceeded the funds available for the pollution-induced cleanup effort and have created legal proceedings that may last for years.

Regularly reported data from the United Nations Inter-Governmental

Maritime Consultative Organization (UNIMCO) indicated that the relative amount of oil spilled from ocean-going tankers has been dropping in recent years. Most of this oil comes from so-called operational pollution rather than dramatic accidents. Operational pollution includes the cleaning of ballast tanks at sea, which is often practiced in contravention of established international regulations. Every crude-oil carrier must regularly flush the residue of previous cargos from its tanks, which are filled with water and used as a ballast once the cargo has been delivered. In theory, instead of discharging this oily water into the sea, 90 percent of the world's oil tankers have special tanks to be used for this expressed purpose. Well-managed ships obey the rules, but many vessels owned by independent tankers are allegedly run in a less-scrupulous manner. Illegal tank flushing becomes more commonplace as the earnings of independent tanker operators dwindle during the current period of worldwide tanker surplus capacity.

Although 80 to 90 percent of the oil pollution at sea comes from operational pollution, and most of this from illegal operations by independents, violations by the major oil companies nevertheless attract most of the public attention, perhaps because of their penchant for naming many of their tankers after themselves. Had the *Amoco Cadiz* been given a different name, then AMOCO (Standard Oil of Indiana) might have been less vulnerable to criticism. Reviews by the trade press of the five dozen major oil spills by tankers in the past fifteen years show that few of these ships were associated with major international petroleum companies.

Oil-well blowouts provide a second major way for the environmental failures of energy companies and governments to make the headlines. The biggest oil spill in history began in June 1979 off the coast of Yucatán, Mexico. An offshore well being drilled by the Mexican state-owned oil firm, Pemex, blew out and began to discharge 30,000 barrels a day of crude oil into the Gulf of Mexico. The oil slick from this well, Ixtoc 1, spread out over more than 300 square miles of water and drifted northwestward into American territorial waters and finally onto the Texas beachfront in the late summer. Pemex, with some assistance from international advisers, was finally able to contain the well in late 1979, but not before more than 2.5 million barrels of crude oil were spilled.

Various cleanup efforts were made by the Mexican government, with the assistance of specialized service companies flown in from the United States. The question of whether contemporary technology can deal promptly with oil-well blowouts in the open ocean remains unanswered. Pemex has been conducting a massive, rapid oil-exploration program in the area of the accident. Consequently because of their haste and the tragedy that occurred, Pemex is now subjected to inquiries regarding its management capabilities and prudence. Lawsuits and claims against several companies have been lodged in U.S. federal courts, totaling more than $350 million.

Reports from the scene indicate that there were problems that could have been solved by better emergency planning. Delays in clearing Mexican customs held up deliveries of cargos of vital imported equipment for days, delaying the use of this equipment to contain the spill. Perhaps no company or government could have coped more quickly with such a disaster. Regardless of where the responsibility for the Pemex fiasco lies specifically, the energy industry as an entity has received worldwide criticism with which it must deal.

The coal industry gets a fair share of criticism for its environmental impact as well. Many years of acid water runoff from underground coal mining has resulted in the destruction of stream life throughout areas of Appalachia; massive piles of mined earth and coal refuse scar the landscape from Pennsylvania to Alabama. Although new laws instituted by federal and state governments in recent years provide for restoration of these lands (including abandoned lands no longer owned by operating coal companies), the public image of the coal industry as a disfigurer of the landscape remains. For these reasons in particular, there has been considerable reluctance to permit the opening of western coal lands for surface mining.

In the West, water shortages and the slower growing seasons contribute to fears that the restoration of lands would be impeded by difficulties in revegetating the surface. The amount of available topsoil in the western states is less than in the East, and the absence of adequate rainfall would certainly make revegetation more difficult.

Business interests might argue that their role in environmental affairs is to respond and not to innovate. Energy suppliers are generally prepared to meet environmental standards if it is possible to pass on the costs of these standards to the end users. If this were not so, they might forgo environmental investments on grounds that it could not be sufficiently profitable to warrant their taking the associated risk. Indeed in the area of environmental protection, most energy companies act as followers rather than leaders. Their public-relations campaigns might sometimes indicate that they would like to be approved of by the public as leaders, but their records suggest that they are more comfortable in a reactive role. Some expenditures on environmental protection do fall into the category of good public relations. Community attitudes can be improved by spending money to enhance the local environment around a mine or an oil refinery, for example. In such a case a firm can benefit from a happier work force and better community acceptance of the installation. Expenditures of this type are made for several reasons, not solely for environmental protection causes.

Many expenditures for environmental improvements are made to remedy pollution only after it has occurred. Tighter adherence to the preventative measures governing such actions as tanker flushing, for example, would be the best hope for upgrading the air, land, and water with minimal costs. However, any comprehensive effort will need to be accompanied by practical economic incentives, especially where sizable costs are involved in the execution of a policy.

Energy Costs

Another way to measure the performance of our energy companies is to consider the relative price changes in energy costs to consumers. It is slightly oversimplified to compare price changes in energy with price changes in consumer goods and services because energy itself is one of the factors determining ultimate cost. Nevertheless the comparison of energy costs can be of value in our understanding of the performance of energy firms. Any measurement of end-user energy costs is clouded by price controls, however. Federal controls have been imposed upon natural gas in varying degrees over the last two decades. In the case of oil-product prices, some controls initially imposed under President Nixon in 1971 were phased out during the 1970s. Regulated prices remain for motor gasoline and certain liquefied gases, such as propane. Insofar as uranium is concerned, that particular mineral fuel was purchased under the terms of a government monopsony until the late 1960s. The military applications for uranium resulted in a series of government actions to control its availability for commercial purposes such as nuclear reactor fuel rods. Only coal has been consistently available at open-market prices, without any major influences on its cost stemming from price controls.

An examination of end-user energy costs is still informative. When viewed against the backdrop of the last few years, clearly energy costs in America have outpaced most other consumer price increases. However, when seen against a time scale of approximately twenty years, there is an interesting equalization in the increased costs of motor gasoline and home heating oil relative to the cost increases for food, housing, clothing, and other consumer goods, as reported by the Bureau of Labor Statistics. Although the decontrol of oil prices and OPEC price hikes does exacerbate the rate of increase, it might be surmised that these increases were overdue in the case of oil and gas, because these are dwindling resources. In addition, some of the price increases relating to mined fuels (coal and uranium) are attributable to the internalizing of costs related to mine safety and workers' health and environmental protection and land reclamation. These costs have been passed on to consumers only recently.

A great deal of the contemporary American style of life requires inexpensive and abundant energy; thus it will be consumers who must choose to what extent this dependence upon energy will be modified in the years ahead. With increased costs for energy will come a few reprieves by the application of new technology to allow improved energy conservation. Energy costs for consumers are heavily influenced by the impact of technological changes. The increasing preference for electrification in the national economy, for example, has been possible through research into electricity generation and transmission on larger scales. Retail and industrial consumers of electricity have also benefited somewhat. New technology has also permitted more energy efficiency in energy-intensive processes, such as electrometallurgy.

Because the percentage of takehome pay spent for fuel and electricity has risen in recent years, the general public has sought reasons why its energy bills have gone up. The energy suppliers—utilities and fossil-fuel producers—are tempting targets but do not warrant the blame to the extent that they have been singled out. Many contributing factors have caused energy costs to rise, not least among them being the power of OPEC to transfer real wealth away from consumers into the hands of oil-exporting countries. The challenge to large energy firms will be to continue to work in the most efficient manner possible to dampen the rise in end-user energy costs, although it is unlikely that they will be in the position to do so singlehandedly. Some transfer-payment mechanism, such as federal income-tax alleviation, seems necessary to ease the impact upon the poor and the elderly.

Electric utilities have also been candidates for popular scorn, but they also have been victims of circumstances to a large degree. Fuel cost increases are passed on by public utilities only with the approval of local and state regulatory commissions. Furthermore public files of review cases indicate that these cost increases are justifiable. The roots of cost increases often lie beyond the direct control of the energy producer or the utility company.

However, from the vantage point of the average citizen, energy costs are as seen in monthly gasoline, light, and heating bills, and the energy-supply system is represented by whomever sends the invoice. Thus frustration and anger are registered with the bearer of the bad news, who is the supplier with whom the consumer has the closest or most recent contact.

Renewable-Energy Resources and Nonenergy Acquisitions

The demand by the general public for faster efforts to improve renewable-energy sources has been only partly met by the private sector. Research and development expenditures on renewable-energy resources are but 1 or 2 percent of the R&D budgets of most large energy-producing companies, a situation that reflects the uncertain near-term economics of most renewable-energy resource technologies, plus solar. Consequently the weight of the efforts to spur renewable-energy resource development has fallen upon the federal government, and in particular the Department of Energy. Spending by the Department of Energy in the area of solar power, for example, is many times such expenditures in the private sector. In fact, the private sector has reacted to the heavy emphasis being made by the federal government by minimizing its own efforts in that area, opting instead to venture into such projects only in response to successful federal endeavors.

Fossil-fuel producers point out that, almost without exception, renewable-energy projects do not offer a commercial return on the outlay, and they would prefer to defer spending until it was more evident that they could earn commercial profits from such ventures. There is a certain irony in this approach, because companies producing fossil fuels in dwindling supply have the long-term option of either leaving the industry or diversifying into new areas of production.

It might seem to make the most sense for these companies to emphasize research into energy alternatives and find them first in order to reap the commercial benefit. To the contrary, some of these firms argue that it is not worth their while to attempt to pioneer in these areas because they can either acquire the necessary expertise by the purchase of success-ful innovative companies or wait until others achieve a breakthrough that they can successfully imitate and perhaps market more efficiently. This approach is not without logic, although it entails certain risks of being left behind.

The public has been particularly sensitive to an unhappy about capital expenditures made by large energy firms for nonenergy purposes. The most notable acquisition, used time and again as an illustration, was the purchase by Mobil Oil Corporation of the Montgomery Ward-Container Corporation of America conglomerate, Marcor. It has also been pointed out often that Gulf Oil made a halfhearted attempt to acquire the Ringling Brothers Barnum and Bailey Circus in the early 1970s. In 1980, Exxon Corporation made a $1.2 billion acquisition of the electric-motor-manufacturing firm, Reliance Electric Company. Exxon held that this particular takeover was an energy-related purchase designed to speed the production and marketing of energy-saving electric motors. Observers remain unconvinced of this claim and view the acquisition as being a straight diversification move by Exxon, in the same vein as the Exxon move into office equipment, including word processors.

Any analysis of outlays made by large energy companies to diversify their activities in nonenergy ways, other than petrochemicals or the manufacture of products deriving directly from fossil fuels, shows that this diversification has been rather modest. According to DOE data, approximately 1 to 2 percent of U.S. energy-company annual capital budgets have gone for purely nonenergy purposes during the past fifteen years. Nevertheless many large firms are so sensitive to the criticism they might receive if they made a serious diversification effort that they have reconsidered such plans. Rising energy prices, of course, have provided the companies with sufficient incentive to continue to emphasize their traditional lines of business, thus decreasing even further any immediate desire to diversify.

Theoretically one could argue that all firms ought to be left to their own devices regarding acquisition. If they choose to leave one line of business and enter another, that is a matter solely for their shareholders to consider and no one else. Petroleum companies in particular have said that if they are restricted specifically to the production of oil and gas, then ultimately, when these reserves run out, they would be forced to liquidate their business. This is a rather exaggerated but popular industry claim. With rising prices making marginal oil and gas deposits now economically viable, there are no immediate prospects for a forced shutdown of any firm due to resource exhaustion.

It appears that the large energy firms may have sincerely tried to achieve public energy goals, but where such efforts have been made, it is because their own private corporate goals overlap considerably with public goals. The private companies have not made undue efforts in the fields of renewable-energy sources, for example. These producers claim there is not enough commercial incentive to warrant their pursuing many of the synthetic-fuel options that might benefit from their energy business expertise, notably the mining of coal, a raw material with significant synthetic fuel possibilities.

Time will help develop a better perspective on how well these private companies are meeting public goals. One measure of their success will be the extent to which they are able to improve their public stature and the rating given them in public-opinion polls. Public attitudes will continue to play an important role in the future of American energy firms. If these organizations are believed to be acting in the best interest of the country, they probably will be allowed to enjoy greater freedom of movement in the economy regarding their commercial activities, including diversification. If they continue to receive a bad performance rating from the general public, warranted or not, they will be subject to increased control by elected officials as the voters use their political power in an attempt to obtain accountability for their own economic discomforts.

It is interesting to consider what would be the reaction if the general public were better informed on energy matters and what political course voters might advocate after evaluating the performance of energy companies. As public information increases, however slowly, the energy firms will become more and more open to unforgiving criticism by an increasingly alert and scrutinizing electorate. Energy-company actions might enhance or deal a severely crippling blow to the trust in their performance by the American public.

8 Public-Policy Alternatives

Although some people decry the absence of a clear national energy policy, it is somewhat misleading to say that no such policy exists. Ultimately policy is what is done, and it is possible, therefore, to identify the components of the existing American energy policy. They include a reliance upon the private sector as the principal vehicle for the location and production of all forms of energy. The single possible exception to this rule is hydroelectric power generated through quasi-public and state-sponsored schemes, such as the Tennessee Valley Authority and the Bonneville Power Administration. The historical role of the national government has been principally a supportive one.

The federal government increasingly has become an important factor in the effort to move toward identifying the indirect costs of energy production and requiring that these costs be internalized into the national energy cost equation. By so doing, the government acts as the guardian of the public interest, helping to ensure that the social costs of energy production, such as environmental impact or health and safety requirements, are properly accounted for before they become an identifiable physical, external diseconomy. This practice leads to higher prices in the short term, but in the long term it avoids dislocations resulting from crash programs designed to remediate past policy shortcomings or negligence.

The American pattern of reliance upon the private sector in energy matters is not much different from that in other segments of our economy. It has its historical roots in the ownership of mineral rights by private citizens, particularly east of the Mississippi River, rather than state ownership, as is the case in many other countries. The centrality of the energy-supply question is whether serious consideration ought to be given to a prompt change in our approach toward energy-supply policy.

The simplest energy-policy option is that of maintaining the status quo. Maintenance of the status quo need not necessarily mean that there would be no changes in the existing laws, regulations, or commercial agreements between firms or between companies and the government. Rather there would be an effort to keep the current balance between the private and public sectors where decision making on investments, research, pricing levels, and other day-to-day commercial decisions are concerned. Ideally the status quo would allow for a harmonious combination of existing social policies regarding the working conditions for energy employees, the continued monitoring of environmental impacts, and a continuing emphasis upon minimizing the political risk from a reliance upon imports for the critical margin of U.S. energy needs.

In particular, the status-quo philosophy assumes that efforts to develop alternative energy sources from solar to geothermal will be made by the private sector without the need for an unusual amount of federal assistance when the economic opportunities are present. It also assumes that there would be no new institution created at the federal or state level to govern energy production and consumption. Energy prices have never been completely free of government price setting. It is possible to imagine that in a status-quo situation, there would be an end to existing price controls on finished petroleum products, crude oil, and natural gas. Such decontrol could be properly phased in over a few years in order to distribute the economic impact that would take place if the controls that were imposed in the past were suddenly lifted.

Perhaps the associated assumptions are too many and too broad. However, as a concept a status-quo scenario offers the opportunity for certain cooperative policies. Not least among the opportunities is that it would more likely than not provide for a climate close to that which most business leaders have expressed in public statements as being optimal for them to discharge their functions as energy suppliers. The status-quo philosophy does not mean there will be a return to a totally laissez-faire economy without any public influence on decisions by energy producers. Such a situation has never existed in the United States and would probably be problematic for the vast majority of energy companies, regardless of the pro-laissez-faire rhetoric so common to industry speeches.

A second major energy-policy alternative would be to continue with a series of gradual modifications in the present government-industry arrangements. This seems to be the direction in which national decision making is going at the present time. Several sorts of modifications come to mind. For example, there might be a much greater federal role in research and development of alternative energy sources or the encouraging of production processes that yield more from existing energy supplies. Examples of such programs might include sponsorship of research into tertiary oil recovery or the production of heavy oils or oil from tar sands and oil shale.

Opportunities for possible greater cooperation between government and the private sector would include research on the production of synthetic gas and liquids from coal. Much discussion on these topics has already taken place, and there have been certain problems in defining just how extensive the federal role should be. In the case of providing loan guarantees or investments in these ventures, there is the question as to whether such guarantees would be poorly received because the return on the equity capital by the private sector might be inadequate to permit decisions for synthetic fuel plants to be justified given alternative investment opportunities.

Another area where modifications in the present arrangements might lead to an energy-supply policy with greater appeal to the general public would be the requiring of an increased disclosure of data by private firms. Some tentative steps in that direction have been taken in recent years and may be continued. This type of arrangement offers a definable measure of control and accountability. Disclosure requirements and data reporting might be one way to demonstrate to the general public and elected officials alike that the business activities of the larger firms are not only accountable but are also conducive to overall energy goals. Sometimes the scale of these companies alone or difficulties with the aggregation of their data present obstacles that hinder any serious effort at analysis of specific components.

Set against the arguments in favor of disclosure of additional information are the costs involved in what may be at heart a public-relations exercise. The monitoring by the Department of Energy and other branches of the federal government has been criticized loudly by private firms as extremely costly to them, and any additional steps to require further disclosures may be expected to receive similar criticism.

A third area of possible modification that might be of interest would be to require that any crude-oil price-decontrol action be tied into a commitment by the oil producers to reinvest the funds in energy-related projects. This plowback concept has been unacceptable to date because the Congress has felt that some of the money raised by oil decontrol ought to be transferred into other segments of the economy, such as the social security funds.

The reason for using part of the receipts of decontrol for purposes and programs not related to energy stems from the popular notion that monetary windfalls would be over and above the total dollar commitment to reinvestment that the energy industry would make. For example, many of the small stripper-well producers do not have active exploration or drilling programs and therefore would not be in a position to reinvest the money in additional wells. For firms of this size, the money received by decontrol would be recycled into the economy in the form of tax cuts or new and expanded existing social and economic programs. That in itself may be a sufficient reason for decontrol. Such an infusion into the economy could conceivably stimulate the creation of demand for more goods and services, thus creating new jobs or renewing others that might otherwise be lost.

An argument against a plowback principle can be made on the grounds that the earnings from decontrol ought to be allowed to be invested according to the dictates of the commercial wisdom of those energy firms receiving the money. This reasoning leaves it to the energy firms to find the most profitable area in which to place these new receipts. In this way, the economy avoids possible opportunity costs that might be incurred if the monies arising from decontrol were forced into less-constructive channels. This policy does not avoid the risk of speculative investments, but most larger energy producers tend to be relatively conservative investors in any case and have usually remained in the extractive industries. The two most widely publicized exceptions are the acquisition by Mobil Oil Corporation of Marcor and in 1979 the Exxon purchase of Reliance Electric.

The fourth broad area of public-policy options calls for hitherto radical alterations. Several proposals in this area have received publicity. Perhaps the most widely discussed have been the divestiture proposals. Vertical divestiture was originally promoted by the late Senator Phil Hart of Michigan and has been pursued vigorously by the Senate Judiciary Subcommittee on Antitrust and Monopoly both during his stewardship of the chair of that committee and under the direction of his successor, Senator Edward M. Kennedy of Massachusetts.

Vertical divestiture would require that large petroleum companies operate in only one area of the oil and gas business, such as exploration and production, or refining, or marketing. Horizontal divestiture would require the limitation of energy firms to dealing with only one of the various energy products. This proposal was directed at those energy firms with expressed interests in uranium, coal, petroleum, and other energy resources and was intended to limit or stop large-firm involvement in the entire energy-fuel spectrum. Preventing such involvement is intended to encourage energy industry competitiveness.

Other proposals made would force divestiture in certain areas of integrated businesses, such as pipelines. The interest in divesting pipelines, in particular, stems from the fact that these are common carriers with regulated rates of return (and are operated, or so it is claimed, in a somewhat different manner from other branches of the oil and gas business). Another radical departure from the present system that has been put forward would limit large-firm eligibility for participation in corporate mergers. Eligibility to merge would be determined by the size of the contemplated merger subject, gross assets involved, and market shares in terms of sales receipts. Senator Kennedy, joined by Senator Howard Metzenbaum of Ohio, has been an advocate of legislation of this type. The intention of these bills is to prevent overconcentration in any one industry. Other proposals seek to limit the investment expenditures of the very large, horizontally integrated energy companies in an effort to prevent them from achieving what is perceived to be an excessively high share of the market. Most of these proposals have been variations on the Sherman Act and the Clayton Act. Opponents charge that existing legislation is adequate to cope with these situations. Proponents have taken the opposite view that additional specific legislation is justified because under current antitrust legislation, adjudication sometimes takes many years to reach resolution and this frustrates and sterilizes the process when there is a need to act quickly.

Still other alternatives include the establishment of a large, federally owned energy corporation either to provide funding for energy proposals or to take a direct part in the exploration for and production of various forms of energy. The concept of an energy bank has also been proposed. The energy bank would lend the revenues derived from taxes on decontrolled oil and gas to those companies wishing to reinvest proceeds in further exploration and production. Funds of this nature could be made available at preferred rates, which might cause a conflict with the private banking industry, to create a positive incentive for additional energy resource outlays.

Somewhat related to this last proposal is the idea of a federally owned energy-producing company because much of the nation's oil-, coal-, and uranium-bearing land is owned by the public and administered by the federal government. Proponents of this idea believe that energy resources on public lands might become usable energy fuel sources if the federal government were to act as the developer of these resources. In the case of offshore oil and gas leases, for example, it was suggested by Senator Phillip Hart of Michigan that the federal government should require the drilling of a series of exploratory wells that would provide additional geological data to those private firms wishing to bid on the rights to these tracts. But what would occur if the federal government's drilling program indicated the acreage to be barren? Perhaps interest in bids and leases would plunge. Therefore it seems better for the federal government not to take part in such a high-risk endeavor. Rather they suggest that the government limit itself to cultivating the appropriate climate for the private sector to take risks with its capital contributed by investors.

Most of the suggestions for radical change involving the federal government as an energy producer have centered on oil and gas rather than on coal and uranium. This is surprising because the end users for most coal and all uranium in the private sector are the electric utilities, which are regulated regional monopolies and are already closely linked to local or central governments. The barriers to entry in coal mining in particular are relatively low, especially on the publicly owned western lands that have surface deposits of coal. Presumably it would be much simpler for the federal government to enter coal mining and sell the output either to organizations like the Tennessee Valley Authority or to investor-owned public utilities.

The relatively low start-up costs, the public ownership of coal-bearing lands, and the guaranteed long-term contracts that could be arranged with utilities are all good, low-risk-related factors that might convince one that a publicly owned coal-producing company could be profitable. The justification for such a company would be another matter. If this public company's role is to compete with the private sector, then it would seem to be counterproductive to the end that its existence would not be a way of increasing the value of publicly owned energy reserves. At this time, suggestions for any federally owned energy-producing company are being held in limbo.

The most radical departure yet noted is the nationalization of all forms of energy production and distribution and marketing. This would be a great step beyond the establishment of a federally controlled energy-producing company. In certain Western European countries, the state has nationalized all coal mines, due largely to the social costs of maintaining a declining industry in regions of those nations that offer few alternative employment opportunities for displaced coal-industry personnel. A parallel situation probably existed in Appalachia in the 1940s and 1950s, but no nationalization decision was made at that time, and the United States deferred the economic care of that isolated area to market forces.

It is unlikely that there will be growth in coal production of a magnitude sufficient to create the pressures necessary for nationalization. Nationalization of the oil and gas sector, on the other hand, seems to be more an emotional response to the perceived excessive power of big business and the desire of the public for some measure of accountability in the energy industry. The replacement of big business with big government may be too simple and too emotional a remedy to a very different and complex problem. New questions regarding the participation and rights of the various states in any new public energy effort undoubtedly would be raised.

An equity interest for a federally owned company in oil, gas, coal, or uranium production on public lands might prove beneficial by improving the practical working knowledge of the Department of Energy and other branches of federal government. However, such a proposal has not been given a serious hearing, and the cost of that experience may be a disincentive. There is, of course, always the option of repealing some of the existing codes and laws that govern energy production in order to provide a less-constrained, freer business environment for energy.

Realistic chances of rolling back legislative initiatives concerning the energy industry involve much the same practical considerations that face any of the other proposals. The one unpredictable factor in the entire energy picture is the role of the public; public perceptions, pleasure or displeasure with the industry, and consumer-voter use of political power will exercise an unpredictable influence on the formation and implementation of any policy.

The dichotomy implicit in the establishment of an energy policy rests in large part on the very volatile and shifting tide of public opinion and, subsequently, public political reaction predicated on those opinions. During 1980 the United States experienced a period of politicized rhetoric that may only cloud knowledge and mystify the public all the more on energy issues. One party to the energy-policy discussion whose voice is ominous only in its absence is that of the large, primarily oil-oriented energy companies. In an industry marked by squabbling and disunity among its members, no counciled voice can speak for the industry. The public, infuriated at OPEC, energy problems, and the price of motor gasoline and home-heating fuel in particular, are further frustrated and baffled by the comparative silence of the major oil companies and other energy producers. There is a clear case of a need for public education concerning energy. However, the energy industry, and in particular the oil companies, have been derelict in that duty. This silence only serves to frustrate consumer-voters all the more. In some quarters of the public this apparent lack of response during a critical time is interpreted as a tacit approval of the current state of affairs.

One may ask just how undereducated the American public is on energy. Some common public beliefs and perceptions on energy have been mentioned earlier. On balance, what the public believes to be the energy story is more accurately described as fallacy and misconception. One example of what the oil industry has had to deal with were charges that the 1979 energy crisis, following the Iranian revolution, was contrived by the oil majors to raise prices and reap excessive profits. These charges were fueled by record profit rates in the industry that same year. The public perception is very heavily biased against big oil. However, both the American Petroleum Institute and the Department of Justice concluded in July 1980 that no evidence exists on which to base any charges of market manipulations by oil firms in 1979. It is probably assuming too much, however, to think that favorable reports on the oil industry by federal, industry, or independent organizations will exonerate the oil industry of the burdensome charges it faces in the minds and attitudes of many Americans.

The public is largely concerned about controlling its destiny. Americans are groping in an effort to obtain an answer to the energy enigma that faces them and threatens their way of life. Therefore they want some type of accountability or control, and therein lies the reason why coal and the utilities suffer less than the oil industry in the often-emotional fervor over energy policy. Because coal reserves exist in massive quantity in the United States and on U.S. government lands there is control; because the public utilities are answerable to the public and the utility rate commissioners, the public perceives some measure of control. However, in the privately operated oil industry there is no such perception; instead there is a perceived lack of control. Thus the silence of the large oil producers, coupled with their relative unwillingness to engage themselves in a program to educate and become allies with the American public, makes the oil industry a prime target for angered consumers.

The oil industry is not replete with angels at its helm, but neither is it overrun with demon directors. For years it was perceived as an efficient industry providing for the majority of America's energy needs at a low cost. Then circumstances changed, and the changes were largely beyond the control of the oil companies. Suddenly they were perceived as proficient only at wringing dollars from the hands of American consumers. There was, coterminously, a desire to put a leash on energy and the related problems of inflation and threats to accustomed ways of life. Thus, if what the large energy companies now face was not predictable, it is at least logical in view of what the American public feels and is consistent with how those feelings are released.

Because previously energy supply and suppliers were marked by stability, there was no reason for the public to be informed about the subject of oil, gas, coal, uranium, solar power, nuclear power, wind power, water power, and so forth. But with the new militancy of Middle Eastern nations and their concern for higher rates of return for their precious depleting economic resource, a good reason for getting interested in energy was at hand.

Exactly how the public gets its data concerning energy is a query that perhaps has as many answers as there are opinionated people in the United States. One thing is quite clear about the process: there has been a great deal of diligent miseducating and learning of misinformation. There are wide rifts between the actual and perceived energy pictures. The public's view of energy is wholly unlike reality. Time and again, Gallup, Yankelovich, and Harris surveys measuring public opinions regarding energy record a set of responses that are quite contrary to the facts. Nevertheless the public does know what it would like: energy derived from nonpolluting, low-risk, renewable, free sources, such as the sun, water, and tide power. This is very admirable and genuine in its expression, but it is also, unfortunately, impracticable and improbable by any yardstick used by informed parties. The public does not know the present or future constructs of the energy scenario facing America. The public envisions nuclear fuels as the primary provider of energy at the turn of the century. Industry experts predict nuclear power's role to be a fraction of the publicly held expectation, a fraction on the order of one fifth or slightly less. The public expects virtually no role for oil in the year 2000, a very optimistic projection perhaps made in spiteful response to OPEC's influences on their previously more tranquil lives. Industry experts project a slightly expanded role for oil by the year 2000. The public also expects a stable role for coal and a vastly expanded role for solar power in the future over the present.

There has been much discussion of the supply alternatives and the problematic perceptions of the public concerning those alternatives. Public reaction in the United States has the capacity to initiate change, a change that may well be inaugurated by a policy selected from a very broad spectrum of available public policies, which themselves are a result of divergent public reactions and perspectives. The United States must mitigate its problems concerning energy perceptions as a first step and only then move to remedy the more serious discomfort caused by the current energy posture by making as learned and as sensible an energy-policy choice as possible.

9 Recommendations and Conclusion

The task of securing long-term energy supplies for the United States is complex and will require many years to be completed. Existing investments in equipment that burns oil and natural gas make it impossible for a rapid change away from these fuel sources to take place without extraordinary capital outlays. Such capital investments would take funds away from other productive sectors of the economy and are, in all likelihood, beyond the financial capability of the nation. But the inability to move rapidly away from any one fuel source need not paralyze our ability to make adaptive changes. A number of incremental changes may have a beneficial cumulative effect if they are made regularly and with adequate specific design to address energy problems. Opportunities to develop solar power by incorporating it into new residential and small commercial buildings would be just one example of a small yet constructive change. A more-rapid growth of solar power would require additional subsidies beyond those tax incentives already in place and might best be postponed until it is clear that there are cost-effective solar-equipment options available for widespread sale and installation.

Coal provides its own set of problems. There is plenty of it and it is relatively cheap to mine, but the costs of shipping and using it are high, particularly the costs associated with preventing widescale environmental contamination. Coal is probably overrated as a short-term source of power for direct burning, but in the medium term—that is, over the next ten years—it could rapidly become the principle source of transportation and space-heating fuel. For this to happen, the technology must be developed for coal to be converted to synthetic liquids and synthetic gases in the quantities that its advocates anticipate.

Abundant quantities of high-BTU synthetic gas derived from American coal could permit the continued use of the existing expensive natural-gas pipeline grid beyond the life span of declining American natural-gas reserves. Substitution of coal-based gas for domestically produced natural gas would be both less expensive and more secure, relative to the importation of liquefied natural gas from Algeria, Indonesia, or other OPEC member countries.

Insofar as crude oil is concerned, there is no need to belabor the point that our current dependence upon significant volumes of foreign petroleum is a hazardous situation. Neither national security nor the balance of payments can tolerate a prolongation of this state of affairs.

The future of nuclear power as a base-load electricity-generating source currently is clouded by the aftermath of the Three Mile Island incident. In the longer term, however, and with the absence of additional incidents such as that in Pennsylvania, one might anticipate that the continued expansion of nuclear power, as a means of taking advantage of this cheap source of energy, would be in the national interest. Despite the enormous public concern about health and related radiation hazards, there have been no civilian fatalities that are directly traceable to the operations of nuclear power plants. The emotional difficulties associated with nuclear power cannot be underrated, and it may be that these factors alone will continue to stymie expansion of this energy source.

No single energy option is without its share of problems. All have their pluses and all have substantial minuses. Because no one energy-supply source stands above the others, it will be necessary to use them all in varying degrees and with different emphases in different parts of the country in order to achieve balanced and sustained economic growth. The ability to decouple the incremental expansion of the national economy from directly proportional increases in energy consumption would assist measurably by postponing the inevitable date at which additional energy resources would be pulled into service. Greater energy efficiency alone, however laudable, cannot indefinitely make up for the need to develop supplemental energy production.

Federal Supporting Role

What national energy policies will permit sustained economic growth by shifting to greater amounts of domestic energy? Will these policies take into account the existence of an established private sector for energy production? Will these energy policies allow the private firms to exist and evolve along with the public regulatory agencies that govern their performance?

One possible option is the proposal to expand the federal role in all aspects of the energy industry far beyond its current scope. Some elected officials and a substantial and growing minority of the general public are fearful that the private sector is unable to cope with the challenges presented in the field of energy supply. Some factions of this minority also believe that the motives of the private sector are questionable and, therefore, private firms should not be trusted with the task. In particular, they worry that private companies place the profit incentive above their obligations to the community. Even if this were true, it is questionable public policy to ask the federal government to step in to supply the incremental funds and personnel necessary for stimulating energy growth.

If such a move were made, the government would only be competing for the same limited labor pool of qualified experienced technicians, business managers, and other professionals. Duplication of effort would exist because both sectors would be purchasing the same goods and services, ranging from oil-field equipment to coal-mining machinery. Furthermore there would be no net gain in productivity from this activity relative to what could be done by the private sector alone, unless the federal government proved able to provide capital that would otherwise be unavailable, or if it were evident that the private sector was otherwise unable to execute its task. It would, of course, be sound public policy to exercise greater federal intervention if high priority were to be placed upon the perceived need for greater state control over energy activities.

At this time, there is no evidence that the energy producers are unable to satisfy their capital requirements independent of any federal help. Indeed the larger firms have record cash flows and are seeking investment outlets. There is an ironic possibility that an inability or unwillingness to place this short-term cash surge into energy-producing ventures will result in greater nonenergy investments and these firms more likely targets for criticism. The remedy to avoid such criticism would seem to be an aggressive, higher-risk effort by the largest energy producers to take on more marginal exploration and development projects. Unless they do so, they will be justly accused of excessive timidity in their investment programming.

Rather than encouraging a more direct federal role in energy production, it would be preferable to have the existing federal role redefined and channeled into frontier technology. For example, a preferred posture for the federal government to take would be to develop its sponsorship of energy research and development in those areas that currently cannot justify investment of sizable quantities of risk capital from the private sector, even under the more aggressive investment strategies.

In energy research and development a variety of experimental ventures currently attract sufficient budget commitments from the private companies. The best place for the federal role to be established is not in these areas but in less-commercial aspects, such as basic research. As research efforts begin to approach the point of commercial application, the role of the state would best be reduced and the function of commercialization handed over to private companies. In the specific case of certain synthetic-fuels applications, it is not easy to identify the transition point at which this changeover would be most efficient. Probably the federal role in synthetic fuel will be much more pervasive than in conventional fuel-production processes because of the abundance of coal on publicly owned land and because of the great expense of the technology for the construction of first-generation plants.

Many alternative routes exist for federal support that fall short of direct federal ownership of facilities and do not require risk-capital investment by the government, (or even minority ownership by the state). For example, it would be possible for synthetic natural gas, produced by gasification of coal, to be priced into pipeline grids at cost plus a reasonable rate of return. Although such a price might be well above the alternative cost of imported liquefied natural gas and would certainly exceed the average price of domestically produced natural gas for some years, an acceptable arrangement may be made whereby synthetic gas would be rolled into the national pipeline grid and the additional costs of this gas borne by all consumers through a sharing of the charges among a number of pipeline companies that would be receiving the gas. Thus there would be a national decision to sponsor the growth of a synthetic fuels industry, while the full cost of paying for the incremental supply of highest-cost synthetic gas need not be borne by a single utility or people within a single state.

Similarly liquids produced from coal could be added to the overall crude-oil supplies of the country on cost plus an agreed profit-margin basis, with the ensuing higher price of crude oil being shared by consumers in the marketplace by a pass-through mechanism. If the synthetic crude-oil refineries distribute this "synfuel" through the regular distributional channels, it might be possible for them to apply this higher cost to all refineries and thereby average out the cost. Other mechanisms can be suggested and developed, all of which would have as their result the averaging out of these higher-cost, coal-based fuels across the entire cost-of-fuel spectrum.

A guarantee of marketability of synthetic gas or liquids provided in this manner might encourage the private sector to accelerate their investment in synthetic-fuels plants, more so than merely guaranteeing federal repayment of loans raised for these ventures because federal loan guarantees do not cover the risk capital that would be represented by the equity invested by the private corporation. The federal government could maintain a supervisory role in order to ensure that the plants constructed under these cost-plus guarantees would be built with sufficient attention to economy and low-cost operation.

Regulatory Function

The regulatory techniques used by government to ensure the accountability of private companies can become a major aid or obstacle to greater energy self-sufficiency. The abnormally great administrative difficulties experienced during the early years of the federal gasoline allocation and price control system during the 1970s are an example of the sorts of obstacles that can be created despite the good intentions of the government. A recurrence of such time wasting and expensive record-keeping procedures must be avoided. Greater experience on the part of public officials will go some way toward ensuring that these administrative problems do not recur. At the same time, monitoring of the energy-producing firms must continue to ensure regulatory compliance on their part. The use of more-streamlined reporting systems on financial and operating data should be encouraged to reduce the overall amount of paperwork required by state and federal government units. The cost of monitoring can outstrip the economic benefits to society, and, in order to prevent this, more-selective use of regulatory compliance procedures must be made. These selective compliance demands should not be confined only to the larger corporations, however.

Although it is true that the opportunities for dramatic corrections, due to dramatic errors, exist to a greater extent when large firms are involved, the frequency of errors in reporting to the government is probably greater in the case of the smaller energy-producing companies. The larger firms can afford the time and talent necessary to ensure (or to thwart) compliance with regulatory processes and the smaller firms cannot. Therefore sometimes the smaller firms do not understand the regulations or do not take time to resolve their questions adequately.

One of the most controversial elements of the federal regulatory apparatus is the recently created Department of Energy. Within the energy industry, in particular, it has been popular to point out that the cost of Department of Energy personnel and programs could be translated into substantial energy price cuts if all of these activities and people were removed from the federal payroll. Other nonindustry critics make use of the notion that the Department of Energy, with all of its resources and personnel and money, cannot produce a single BTU of energy. Many in and out of the energy industry would prefer to see the Department of Energy disbanded. But on balance, it does not seem to be either feasible or practical for this to happen. The Department of Energy clearly needs more time to mature and evolve into an impartial administrative agency capable of exercising more-sensitive control and liaison with the energy industries. The antagonistic attitudes between federal regulators and their counterparts in the private sector must be mitigated. This cannot be achieved until there is enough mutual respect to allow for a patient hearing of the points of view held by the several parties. Perhaps the passage of time will achieve this more constructive sense of community among energy professionals in the United States. The Department of Energy is young and makes many mistakes, but it has also shown the capacity to learn and there are well-founded expectations for improvements. The benefits to the nation of a Department of Energy with the skills and imagination of similar agencies in Western European countries would be very great.

Encouragement for Smaller Firms

The emphasis that the media place by the larger energy producers—notably the multinational oil companies—make it easy to ignore the fact that the spine of national energy-production efforts consists of many small companies. These small companies have and will continue to command a central role in meeting national energy-supply objectives. They deserve continued encouragement to execute this job. The nature of this encouragement need not go so far as the recent program of entitlements to small refiners, which allowed a number of inefficiently small oil refineries to be built and to prosper. This situation arose because of a federal scheme that equalized crude-oil costs among refiners, a state of affairs that is due to end in October 1981 when price controls on domestic crude oil are to expire. The best way for state and national authorities to encourage smaller firms might be to structure incentives more along the lines of small business provisions, as allowed for in federal contracting. For example, there may be a set-aside provision for small businesses in the assignment of federal lands containing energy minerals, oil, and gas.

For many smaller oil and gas companies, there is no need to provide special incentives for them to take part in more-expensive exploration ventures, such as in the Gulf of Mexico or in Alaska. These companies have ample opportunity for in-fill and step-out drilling in the established oil-producing provinces of the contiguous forty-eight states. Furthermore there is little reason to expect that they would wish to assume unnecessary additional risks when there are plenty of lower-risk opportunities available to them. Yet if necessary or if choice should warrant, it should be possible to create some opportunities for these firms to take an interest in a small share of these high-risk exploration projects, if they were so inclined. Beyond the subject of exploration opportunities, smaller oil-producing firms are more immediately concerned about ready access to pipeline networks in order to ship crude oil and natural gas at competitive rates.

Economies of Scale

One of the great problems of the next few years will be to determine whether the largest energy-producing companies have reached or passed a point at which further economies of scale are possible. The answer to the question of scale requires a sociological reply as well as an economic one.

Limitless growth clearly brings with it the seed of its own destruction. Large firms are not immune to business errors, and when such mistakes cause the business to collapse, the crash is very large. Indeed there is a history of such incidents befalling the largest American companies. The bankruptcy of the eastern railroads and the difficulties of the American steel and automotive industries need only be cited to make this point. Size alone is no guarantee of efficiency.

Should there be controls on the growth of the energy companies? Should they be required to concentrate all of their efforts in the exploitation of energy, or should they be allowed to diversify and develop alternative lines of business? Classical economists would argue that they should be entitled to diversify as they see fit. They hold that these firms are privately funded by investors and are thereby entitled to the same range of options as other companies, in other lines of business, which may choose to diversify as they wish. Furthermore if energy firms were to choose to divest themselves of their energy-producing interests, other nonenergy firms presumably would find it attractive to take up the energy companies' former positions.

Alternatively a would-be energy producer could make a de novo entry. It is not particularly difficult to become an energy producer, aside from the admittedly prohibitive costs of setting up business in a geographically remote and hostile region, such as is found in the Arctic seas. The science and technology are well established, and the necessary people and materials can be acquired by bidding for personnel and goods already in the marketplace. Freedom of choice in business endeavors has served the United States well over the years, and there is no reason to exclude the energy companies from enjoying these same privileges.

Accepting this point of view does not require simultaneous granting to the energy companies a license to diversify by acquisition and merger without some limitations. Growth for growth's sake is an outmoded concept. Therefore the efforts to limit the merger between firms over a certain size have merit and need not be discouraged. The thresholds at which any limitations might apply need to be reexamined regularly in the light of changing business and social conditions.

Outlook

The outlook seems to be for a period of continued inefficient groping toward a rebuilding of confidence between the private sector and the regulatory agencies of the state and federal government. Considerable damage was done during the 1970s through recriminations leveled at the private sector in the wake of the rapid transfer of economic power away from the United States to the oil-supplying countries, a process that has accelerated since 1973. The search for scapegoats has been costly, but that period now seems to be fading, and the prospects of some kind of renewed cooperation between industry and government, marked by an ability and willingness to work together toward the national goal of reduced energy-import dependence, has finally begun. The 1980s will contain its share of ill-timed energy shocks that will disrupt any efforts to move away from the current imbalanced overdependence upon imported oil and gas. Inter-regional tensions among energy have and have-not states may worsen. Nevertheless the framework for cooperative planning and decision making seems to be in place. The challenge ahead will be to use this framework and the limited time at our disposal to make more-rapid progress than in the past.

Bibliography

Adelman, M.A. *The World Petroleum Market.* Baltimore: Johns Hopkins University Press, 1972.

American Nuclear Society and U.S. Department of Energy. *Proceedings of the Topical Symposium on Uranium Resources — An International Assessment.* Las Vegas: American Nuclear Society, 1978.

American Petroleum Institute. *Basic Petroleum Data Book.* 4th printing. Washington, D.C.: American Petroleum Institute, 1978.

Askari, H.G., Ruefli, T.W., Kennedy, M.P. *Horizontal Divestiture of Energy Companies and Alternative Policies.* Austin: University of Texas, Graduate School of Business, 1977.

Atwood, J., Hersh, A., Newport, J. *Energy Diversification by Firms in the United States.* Washington, D.C.: American Petroleum Institute, 1978.

Blair, J. *The Control of Oil.* New York: Vintage Books, 1978.

British Petroleum Company, Ltd. *BP Statistical Review of the World Oil Industry.* London: British Petroleum Company, Ltd., various years.

Chase Manhattan Bank, N.A. *Capital Investments of the World Petroleum Industry.* New York: Chase Manhattan Bank, various years.

——. *Financial Analysis of a Group of Petroleum Companies.* New York: Chase Manhattan Bank, various years.

Congressional Research Service. *Are We Running Out? A Perspective on Resource Scarcity.* Washington, D.C.: Library of Congress, 1978.

——. *Centralized vs. Decentralized Energy Systems: Diverging or Parallel Roads?* Washington, D.C.: Library of Congress, 1979.

——. *Project Interdependence: U.S. and World Energy Outlook through 1990.* Washington, D.C.: Library of Congress, 1977.

Cowan, E. "Carter Bids to Curb Oil Companies." *The New York Times,* July 20, 1979, pp. D1-2.

Dafter, R. "Public Illusions About Energy." *Financial Times,* London: June 4, 1980, p. 19.

Duchesneau, T.D. *Competition in the U.S. Energy Industry.* Cambridge, Mass.: Ballinger Publishing Company, 1975.

Executive Office of the President, Energy Policy and Planning. *The National Energy Plan.* Washington, D.C.: U.S. Government Printing Office, April 29, 1977.

Ezra, D. *Coal and Energy.* New York: John Wiley & Sons, Inc., 1978.

Gordon, R.L. *Economic Assessment of Coal Supply: An Assessment of Existing Studies.* Palo Alto, Calif.: Electric Power Research Institute. Vol. 1, 1975, Vol. 2, 1977.

Jacoby, N.H. *Multinational Oil.* New York: Macmillan Publishing Company, 1974.

Johnson, W.A., Messick, R.E., VanVactor, S., and Wyant, R.E. *Competition in the Oil Industry.* Washington, D.C.: George Washington University, 1976.

Landsberg, H.H. *Energy—The Next Twenty Years.* A Report Sponsored by the Ford Foundation. Cambridge, Mass.: Ballinger Publishing Company, 1979.

Lantzke, U. "The OECD and Its International Oil Agency." *The Oil Crisis.* New York: W.W. Norton and Company, 1976.

Lovins, A. *Soft Energy Paths: Toward A Durable Peace.* New York: Harper & Row, 1977.

Meadows, D.L. *Fallacies that Block the Search for an Appropriate Energy Plan.* Hanover, N.H.: Dartmouth Research Program on Technology and Public Policy, 1979.

Meadows, E. "Why the Oil Companies Are Coming Up Dry in Their Public Relations." *Fortune,* July 30, 1979, pp. 54–57.

Mendershausen, H. *Coping with the Oil Crisis.* Resources for the Future Inc. Baltimore: Johns Hopkins University Press, 1976.

Mitchell, E.J., ed. *Horizontal Divestiture in the Oil Industry.* Washington, D.C.: American Enterprise Institute, 1978.

Mitchell, E.J., ed. *Vertical Integration in the Oil Industry.* Washington, D.C.: American Enterprise Institute, 1976.

Mulholland, J.P. Haring, J., Martin, S. *An Analysis of Competitive Structure in the Uranium Supply Industry.* Washington, D.C.: Federal Trade Commission, 1979.

Mulholland, J.P. and Webbink, D.W. *Concentration Levels and Trends in the Energy Sector of the U.S. Economy.* Washington, D.C.: Federal Trade Commission, 1974.

National Research Council, Committee on Nuclear and Alternative Energy Systems. Demand and Conservation Panel. *Alternative Energy Demand Futures to 2010.* Washington, D.C.: National Academy of Sciences, 1979.

———. Supply and Delivery Panel. *U.S. Energy Supply Prospects to 2010.* Washington, D.C.: National Academy of Sciences, 1979.

New York Times. "Transcripts of the President's News Conference on Foreign and Domestic Matters." October 14, 1977, p. A 16.

Oil and Gas Journal, "Shell Barely Holds Top Gasoline Spot." May 7, 1979, pp. 52, 54.

———. "Demonstrators for Lower Oil Prices Misdirect their Fire." September 17, 1979.

Portney, P.R., ed. *Current Issues in U.S. Environment Policy.* Baltimore: Johns Hopkins University Press, 1978.

Regens, J.L., ed. *Energy Issues and Options,* Athens, Ga.: University of Georgia, Institute of Government, 1979.

Rothberg, P., Crane, L., et al. *Synthetic Fuels from Coal: Status and Outlook of Coal Gasification and Liquefaction.* Washington, D.C.: Congressional Research Service, Library of Congress, 1979.

Rouhani, F. *A History of OPEC.* New York: Praeger, 1971.

Rustow, D.A. *OPEC: Success and Prospects.* New York: New York University Press, 1976.

Safer, A.E. *International Oil Policy.* Lexington, Mass.: Lexington Books, D.C. Heath and Company, 1979.

Sowell, E. and Brannan, M. *Market Shares and Individual Company Data for U.S. Energy Markets: 1950– 1977.* Washington, D.C.: American Petroleum Institute, 1978.

Stobaugh, R. and Yergin, D. *Energy Future.* New York: Random House, 1979.

Teece, D.J. *Vertical Integration and Vertical Divestiture in the U.S. Oil Industry.* Stanford, Calif.: Stanford University Institute for Energy Studies, 1976.

Tilton, J.E. *The Future of Nonfuel Minerals.* Washington, D.C.: The Brookings Institution, 1977.

Trager, F.N., ed. *Oil, Divestiture and National Security.* New York: Crane, Russak & Company, 1977.

Tugendhat, C. *The Multinationals.* New York: Random House, 1972.

U.S. Congress. House Committee on the Judiciary. Subcommittee on Monopolies and Commercial Law. *Competitive Aspects of Oil Company Expansion into Other Energy Sources.* Washington, D.C., 1978.

——. House Committee on Science and Technology. Subcommittee on Advanced Energy Technologies. *Alternative Energy Conservation Strategies—* An Economic Appraisal. Washington, D.C., 1978.

——. House Committee on Ways and Means. *Crude Oil Windfall Profits Tax Act of 1979.* Washington, D.C., H.R. 3919.

——. Senate Committee on Energy and Natural Resources. *Synthetic Fuels from Coal: Status and Outlook of Coal Gasification and Liquefaction.* Washington, D.C., 1979.

——. Senate Committee on Energy and Natural Resources. Subcommittee on Energy Research and Development. *Petroleum Industry Involvement in Alternative Sources of Energy.* Washington, D.C., 1977.

——. Senate Committee on the Judiciary. Subcommittee on Antitrust and Monopoly. *The Energy Industry Competition and Development Act of 1977.* Washington, D.C., S. 1927.

——. Senate Committee on the Judiciary. Subcommittee on Antitrust and Monopoly. *Interfuel Competition.* Washington, D.C., 1975.

——. Senate Committee on the Judiciary. Subcommittee on Antitrust and Monopoly. *The Petroleum Industry.* Washington, D.C., Part I: 1975, Part II: 1976, Part III: 1976.

——. Senate Committee on the Judiciary. *The Petroleum Industry: S. 2387.* Washington, D.C., 1976.

——. Senate Committee on the Judiciary. *Petroleum Industry Competition Act of 1976.* Washington, D.C., Parts I and II: 1976.

U.S. Department of Energy. *Monthly Energy Statistics.* Washington, D.C.: U.S. Department of Energy, various issues.

——. Energy Information Administration. Annual Report to Congress— 1979, v. 2. Washington, D.C.: Department of Energy (DOE/ EIA-0173 (79)/2), 1980.

——. *National Energy Plan II: Report to Congress.* Washington, D.C.: Department of Energy, 1979.

U.S. Geological Survey, *Geological Estimates of Undiscovered Recoverable Oil and Gas Resources in the United States* (U.S.G.S. Circular 725). Washington, D.C.: Department of the Interior, 1975.

The Uranium Institute. *Uranium and Nuclear Energy: Fourth International Symposium.* London: Mining Journal Books, 1979.

Vernon, R., "Storm Over the Multinationals: Problems and Prospects." *Foreign Affairs* vol. 55, no. 2, pp. 243-262.

——. "Multinational Enterprise and National Governments: Exploration of an Uneasy Relationship.", *Columbia Journal of World Business* vol. DI, no. 2, pp. 9-16.

Index

Index

About the Author

William G. Prast is an international energy economist with a special interest in public-policy studies. He received the B.S. and M.S. degrees in petroleum engineering and the Ph.D. in mineral economics. Dr. Prast is president of Atlantis Energy and Mineral Economic Services, Inc., New York, a consulting firm specializing in investment advisory services and policy analysis. Prior to establishing Atlantis, he was for fifteen years with Conoco Inc., holding various managerial posts in the United Kingdom. Dr. Prast is adjunct professor in the Krumb School of Mines at Columbia University and has written extensively on topical aspects of the international energy and minerals industries.